Much love to my dear
friend Azima (Harpo)
from her great admirer

Abi - Ru Shinzon

Suluk 2007

THE NEWTON SERIES
Ancient Wisdom in the Modern World
Volume Two

THE SOVEREIGN SOUL
Sufism: A Path for Today
by Phillip Gowins

THE SOVEREIGN SOUL

Sufism: A Path for Today

By Phillip Gowins

New Paradigm Books Boca Raton 2006

NEW
PARADIGM
BOOKS

New Paradigm Books
22491 Vistawood Way
Boca Raton, FL 33428
Tel.: (561) 482-5971 / Toll-Free: (800) 808-5179
FAX: (561) 852-8322
Email: <darbyc@earthlink.net>
Website: <http://www.newpara.com>

The Newton Series:
Ancient Wisdom in the Modern World
Volume 2
The Sovereign Soul:
Sufism: A Path for Today
By Phillip Gowins. Copyright © 2006 Phillip Gowins. All rights reserved. This book, or parts thereof, may not be reproduced in any form without permission.

The author wishes to thank the Sufi Order International for permission to quote from the writings of Hazrat Inayat Khan and Vilayat Inayat Khan.

Cover design by Peri Poloni-Gabriel, Knockout Design
<http://www.knockoutbooks.com>

QP Publication Edition: July 2006.

New Paradigm Books ISBN   1-892138-10-7
New Paradigm Books EAN   978-1-892138-10-1
Library of Congress Control Number: 2006928832

10 9 8 7 6 5 4 3 2 1

To the Memory of

Pir Vilayat Inayat Khan

My Teacher and My Friend

TABLE OF CONTENTS

Acknowledgements

Some fifteen years ago, I had picked up my teacher, Pir Vilayat Inayat Khan, at the airport and was taking him into New York City. We were chatting about nothing much, as we often did, when he suddenly turned to me and said, almost commanded, "Write a book!"

I distinctly remember turning to look at him in disbelief, thinking he was pushing his luck asking me to write a book. After all, books on Sufism are written by scholars or by men and women at his level. But, a few years later, acting on an inner impulse that I am sure he planted, I wrote my first tentative paragraphs and slowly began to compose.

As the book grew, it seemed to take on a life of its own, and I was its helpless but willing servant—an experience I know is shared by many other writers and artists. I do not think I was really compelled, as Pir Vilayat was a great believer in free will. Besides his apparent and surprising trust in me to do something useful, I do know that I would never have completed the book were it not for a few very special people. First and foremost is my wife, Majida Dawn Gowins, who continually kept telling me to keep on writing and who put up with my typing on the computer at five in the morning. I am grateful for the constant encouragement of my beloved friend Zumurrud Butta, who made me believe that I just might have something to say. Then there are the people who read through the first drafts and gave me the feedback that I needed to keep going: my stepdaughter Uriel Belinda Gray, my friends Siddiqi Heather Ferraro and Roshan Jennifer Ferraro, and Muhasaba Molly Wender and Gabrielle Weeks. I owe a debt of gratitude to Abi-Ru Shirzan, who wrote the preface and did the final style checking on the manuscript. Lastly comes John Chambers, initially a stranger and now a friend, who believed in the book and agreed to publish *The Sovereign Soul*.

Preface

Sufis tend to emphasize that, as a form of communication, words are too limited to have great value. Even the poet Rumi, whose thirty thousand verses top American bestseller lists seven hundred and fifty years after his death, scoffed at the ability of words to convey "that Reality." A Sufi book, then, is something of a paradox. It is a collection of words about something that cannot be conveyed in words. Phillip Gowins, in this insightful personal narrative, acknowledges as much, more than once.

Why read it, then? Rumi, asked a similar question, replied, "Words set you searching. They are not the objects of your quest. . . Words are like glimpsing movement far in the distance. You start in that direction to see better." And so, in reading the words that follow, you set your feet on a trail.

Just the act of picking up this book and glancing at it suggests that you are a seeker. You may have been intrigued by its title and wanted to know more. You may even have heard about Sufis and wondered who they are.

Like so much else encountered on the Sufi Path, the word *Sufi* itself is mysterious in its origin and manifold in its meanings. Some are convinced that the word has its origins in the Arabic term for the coarse woolen cloaks that early seekers wore; others insist that it comes from the Arabic word for the verandas where those closest to Mohammad fervently prayed. Another derivation suggests a common ancestry with the Greek *sophia*, or wisdom. Many prefer to look to *saaf*, or purity, to explain the name.

For Sufis, however, such debates are of only mild interest. It is Being that captivates their attention.

The automatic and unthinking response of many scholars is to categorize Sufis as Islamic mystics. Like many "definitions" connected with the Sufi Path, this one has elements of truth, yet is not completely true. For many centuries, Sufis—or, as they are alternately known, dervishes—have found the warmest welcome in countries and areas that have embraced Islam, as a quick glance at the names of Sufi teachers and saints demonstrates. While many Sufis are devout, observant, and orthodox Muslims, many others, however, are less orthodox. Still others are adherents of other religions. Sufis frequently point out that, although the name "Sufi" is associated with the followers of the Prophet Mohammad, spiritual seekers known by other names both predated him and greeted him once he arrived. The Sufi Way is not a religion or a component of a religion but the heart of all religions and spiritualities. So far is it from dogma that Sufi teachers often express their discomfort with the term "Sufism," which suggests a rigid and fixed doctrine.

It is also very common for Sufi teachers to spend considerable time and energy explaining other things that the Sufi Path is NOT. In different ways, the masters all emphasize that Sufis offer no one-size-fits-all philosophy, no shalt and shalt-not commandments, no guarantees, and no clearly delineated goal. As *The Sovereign Soul* demonstrates, progress on the Path demands a constellation of qualities—commitment, authenticity, patience, surrender, love, and yearning, among others—but the evocation and balance of these characteristics is unique for each individual.

Because there is no equivalent of a catechism or a creed for Sufis, teachers are essential. The very presence of a teacher helps a student progress spiritually, and much teaching is transmitted nonverbally. Because teachers are channels for divine light, initiates of Sufi orders preserve knowledge of the *silsila*, or chain of transmission, from one teacher to the next. The silsila can be likened to an electrical cord that carries the charge from the source of power to a particular lamp. Because Sufis adapt to conditions and populations that vary and change, however, there are many groups, or orders, of Sufis. Orders have originated in many locales and are found all over the world. Each order has its own "personality" and flavor, coming as it does from a particular place and the interpretations of individual teachers. Just as each lamp in a house can appear different and shed light in its own way, though, each order draws on the one source of power acknowledged by all Sufis: Divine Love. A Sufi may be affiliated with the Naqshbandi Order, or the Ni'amatullah, Mevlevi, Qadiri, Rifa'i, Bektashi, Tijani, Shadhili, or one of many others. The distinctions among Sufis are considered much less significant than their similarities.

The author of the present book is part of the Sufi Order International, a Chisti branch of the Sufi Path. The silsila of this order, like those of all genuine Sufi orders, begins with the Divine One, followed by the Angel Jibra'il, or Gabriel, and then the Prophet Mohammad and the blessed Ali. It proceeds to a thirteenth-century Syrian saint who initiated Afghanis in the Sufi Way and from there to a series of saints who migrated to Gujarat, India and taught there for hundreds of years.

In 1910, an initiate of this order, under instructions from his own spiritual teacher, brought the Sufi Message to the West. Hazrat Inayat Khan thus began a great spiritual awakening and transformation of those who heard him speak and read his writings. In the span of only seventeen years, Pir-o-Murshid (Leader and Teacher) Hazrat (Holy Presence) Inayat Khan began the Sufi Movement in North America and Europe. A gifted and celebrated master of Indian classical music, he sacrificed his composing and performing to teach tolerance, love, unity, and consciousness. Upon his early death, his son Pir Vilayat Khan succeeded him. In 2000, Hazrat Inayat Khan's grandson, Pir Zia Inayat Khan, assumed leadership of the Sufi Order International. (Among his many other activities, Pir Zia has founded and heads a mystic school, the Suluk Academy, in New Lebanon, New York.)

These pirs are the teachers of whom Phillip Gowins writes. His many years of close communion with Pir Vilayat and his decades of teaching and leadership enable him to write from experience and first-hand knowledge about *tasawwuf*, the Sufi Path.

The way in which he writes is identifiably Sufi. Like Rumi's *Masnavi* and Sa'adi's *Gulistan* (and many other Sufi works), this book appears to have very little pattern. On the surface, it seems to be a fascinating tangle of anecdotes, autobiography, philosophy, practices, references, reflections, musings, and meanderings. A casual reader might find the organization oddly elastic, or even suspect that there is very little organization at all.

The casual reader would be mistaken. As Sufis constantly remind us, there's a lot going on below, above, and beyond the surface. There is a jazzy rhythm to this writing that echoes the unpredictable syncopation of life itself. Our attention seems to be drawn first here, to a memory of a guide, then here, to a recollection of a student's frustrations, then there to something Pir Vilayat said on retreat. In trying to follow the apparent digressions and circular stories, we may feel that we are losing our concentration, our grip on what we are being told. We may become anxious about whether we are getting the point.

And that, of course, is precisely the point—that we can let go and surrender to a pattern that we may not easily discern, that we can give up control and linear logic and just immerse ourselves in what is given. Phillip Gowins invites us along for a ride and tells us that we don't need to drive the car, that we can admire the scenery and enjoy the journey. Like the very best storytellers, he keeps us so spellbound that we don't worry about the bumps in the road and the bends in the tale. It may be some time before we even notice that, though he sits in the driver's seat, his hands seldom grip the wheel. There is a pattern in this book—but it is not imposed by either reader or writer. It emerges.

As you begin the wonderful trip through these pages, though, you don't really need to map out where you are going. It is needless to worry about patterns or fret about what exactly a Sufi is. Just glimpse the movement far in the distance, as Rumi suggested. Let the words set you searching.

Debra Bunch Ghosh   (Abi-Ru Shirzan)
November, 2005

THE SOVEREIGN SOUL

Sufism: A Path for Today

Introduction

Riding on the horse of hope,
Holding in my hand the rein of courage,
Clad in the armor of patience,
And the helmet of endurance on my head,
I started on my journey to the land of love.
    - HAZRAT INAYAT KHAN

One night when I was twenty-six, I was lying in bed next to my wife (my first wife, I mean), waiting to fall asleep, when a sensation like a traveling electric shock swept down through my body.

I thought nothing of it until it happened again. It happened a third time, then kept on happening at three-or four-second intervals. It was like a pulsing hoop of energy that started at my head and coursed down through my entire body—like a wave front hitting the beach again and again.

I was puzzled, then alarmed, then frightened, then really scared, until I was begging it to stop. But it just went on and on. It seemed to be happening on some psychic level, maybe in my aura (though I didn't know what an aura was then), and despite my pleading I remember thinking that it was really all right, that no actual harm was being done to me. And then, just when I thought it was over, another wave came crashing down, exploding, enlivening, energizing me. Then it stopped.

I lay there for a long time, not daring to sleep for fear the energy would sneak up on me again. At the same time I was amazed, even pleased that something unusual had happened to me, because nothing much had ever happened to me in my life before. But I was exhausted and I soon fell asleep. My wife, lying beside me, never stirred.

When I got up the next morning I went into the bathroom to look at myself in the mirror for some sign of change—a pentagram carved into my forehead, perhaps, or a white streak running down the middle of my hair—some sign I hadn't just dreamt this shimmering wave of energy that had kept me awake and affected me in some unknown but possibly profound way. But I saw nothing, no outward sign, only the same lazy old frightened loser who looked back at me from the mirror every day, the same old frightened failure who was well on his way to joining the league of disappointed unpleasant old men who sit in badly lit taverns in cities all over the world telling each other lies about their adventurous youth.

The phenomenon did not repeat itself the next night and it never happened again. But I thought that if what had happened had really happened, then something had to have changed inside me, or in my life—hadn't it?

Later, I would come to view this experience as a wakeup call, my spiritual alarm clock going off.

For a long time I had strongly suspected that I was not a very interesting or likable person, certainly not one interesting enough to attract a bizarre and unknown energy field in the middle of the night. In those days I was mystified by life, clueless, adrift, frightened, insecure, but intelligent. I knew I was smart. I just didn't know what at. College didn't interest me. I had a wife I didn't know how to be with and a son I didn't know what to do with. I didn't know how to express affection or joy or any emotion at all except perhaps the disdain and contempt that come from the false pride people put on when what they really feel is that they are unworthy. My opinions were as changeable as the wind, except for two things: I liked sex (that was a firm opinion), but I suspected I wasn't very good at it (a common enough guy terror, I suppose), and I had just discovered pot, which I thought was totally wonderful (remember, we're talking 1970 here). How I envied people who had firm convictions and expressed them unequivocally! Any authentic opinions I had about life and the world were so totally hidden within me as to be unknown even to myself.

The next stage in my spiritual odyssey (though I didn't yet know I was on one) took place when I was sitting in a state of reverie on the living room floor of our house in Oregon (I may have been stoned), gazing out the window at a very tall, very green pine tree. I was thinking about how the world was a big objective whole unto itself and not just the series of disconnected perceptions we all have of it. This way of looking at things may be very familiar to some, but it was new to me at the time, and I was much enamored of it. It had also dawned on me that this objective whole might be a conscious, living entity—alive like myself—and that if I wanted to be of use to this dynamic, living world, then I should seriously dedicate myself to being a conscious, aware part of its single-entity aliveness.

And then, suddenly, I took a vow to whatever cosmic forces rule. I vowed that whatever I could do or however those forces could use me to be of service to the world, I would be at their disposal.

This was something that came from so deep inside me that it surprised even me. But I knew I truly meant it.

Whatever cosmic forces were listening must have taken me seriously, because a few months later my life completely fell apart. I now know that this happened because I'd triggered a crucial change in myself that demanded nothing less than the total dismantling of the life I'd lived up till then. What shape did this falling apart take? My wife left me and took the children with her. There followed a series of misadventures at the end of which I found myself on the other side of the U.S.A., in Boston, living in my brother's spare room.

It had taken two years for all this unpleasantness to unfold. As it did, I was constantly aware in the back of my mind that the vow I'd made to the cosmos was the precipitating factor, and I couldn't help telling myself that if this one simple vow could make so much happen, then what might I be able to accomplish if I could place at the service of God a serene mind and not my present confused consciousness?

I persisted in this distressed and aimless state for another couple of years. From time to time I leafed idly through books on spirituality or meditation or even stranger aspects of esoteric thought. Sometimes I made attempts to meditate. I attended seminars, some of them given by people who certainly knew what they were talking about, though I was not prepared to accept that at the time.

Then, one night, I looked into the mirror again. This time, though, it was the mirror of my soul. And I had a third experience. There was nothing esoteric or paranormal about it. It was a humiliating sort of experience, one we all have from time to time. I'd been reflecting on some concepts having to do with spirituality and thinking how clever I was to be able to understand the concepts I was reflecting on. All of a sudden my thoughts coalesced into a single reproach directed at myself. It was, "And just who do you think you are?"

I didn't like what I was seeing in my mind's eye. It was ugly. I saw self-pity and cowardice and just about every other negative quality attributable to man. I saw pettiness and a lack of sympathy for others. Seeing this was hardly calculated to make me feel good. But I also saw that I hardly even knew how to feel good.

I decided it was time for a beer, but I couldn't find one in the house. So instead I took another vow, this time to change this personality of mine. I took a vow never to forget what I had seen in myself that night and to alter every aspect of it.

I didn't go to a therapist. That's not a step I wanted, or I would ever want, to take. Call it a personal quirk. Instead, I began to develop the spiritual techniques that I still use today, techniques that work for me—techniques that aren't magical, that can't be described glibly, and that consist of a lot of steady plodding work.

To resume my narration: We are now in February 1979, and, as I've said, I was living in my brother's spare room in Boston. In Boston, I continued what had now actually become my spiritual search. It wasn't entirely spiritual. One of the things I was in search of was a girl friend, and I found one.

This girl friend led me to my teacher.

One day we walked into a lecture room in the Sufi Center in mid-town Boston to listen to a talk by Pir Vilayat Inayat Khan, spiritual head of the Sufi Order International.

When I caught my first glimpse of Pir Vilayat, I knew I had come home.

Pir Vilayat Inayat Khan was sixty-three at the time. I saw, seated before me on a raised dais, a short man with fierce black eyes, a carefully trimmed white beard, and a vigorous shock of hair brushed back from his forehead. The description I give is an inadequate one—and it is mostly an irrelevant one, since it describes the physical Pir Vilayat. What I really picked up on was a wave of energy—an oddly familiar wave of energy—that frightened the bejesus out of me and would continue to do so for quite some time.

That afternoon, Pir Vilayat spoke on the subject of meditation. I listened raptly. I had never met anyone with so sharp a mind combined with so compassionate a being. I felt compelled to follow him. Three months later, I underwent *Bayat*, "the taking of hands"—the Sufi ceremony of commitment. Now I was a Sufi. Of course, you do not *become* a Sufi. You *are* a Sufi, from the moment you commit yourself to the order. Your Sufihood, which was always there, manifests itself more and more.

By the time of my Bayat, I had learned much about my teacher and his place in Sufism. Here's an outline.

Pir Vilayat was the son and successor of a great spiritual leader generally called Murshid, or Teacher. This teacher, Hazrat Inayat Khan, had been born into a family of distinguished Indian classical musicians in Baroda, India, in 1882. At the height of his musical career, when he was already celebrated for his talent, Murshid had been instructed by his own spiritual teacher to take the Sufi message into the West. He had set out on this mission in 1910. During the next 16 years, he taught throughout Europe and the United States. The organization he founded was known, after his death in 1927, as the International Sufi Movement in Europe and the Sufi Order International in America.

Murshid's children were extraordinary as well. For instance, the oldest child, Noor-un-Nisa, was a heroine of the French Resistance, better known by her code name Madeleine. Several books have been written (the best known is *A Man Called Intrepid*) describing her perilous service as a link between the British War Office and the French underground. Her transmissions played a key role in enabling the Allies to land in Normandy on D-Day. Betrayed by a comrade, she was ultimately tortured and executed at Dachau.

Pir Vilayat himself had known from earliest childhood that he was expected to continue his father's work. In keeping with Sufi tradition, however, he was educated in "worldly" knowledge and skills as well as "mystical" lore. He studied philosophy and psychology at the Sorbonne, composition and cello at the Ecole Normale de Musique in Paris, and continued to do postgraduate work at Oxford

University. During the Second World War, he served as an officer in the Royal British Navy, and was assigned to a minesweeper on the D-Day invasion that Noor-un-Nisa's information had helped make possible. He was no ivory tower academic distanced from real life.

After the war, Pir Vilayat submitted to rigorous spiritual training from teachers throughout India and the Middle East. He learned from Hindus, Buddhists, Jews, Christians, Muslims—and, of course, the many flavors of Sufis—and then worked to integrate the knowledge he attained. On June 17, 2004, not long before this book was completed, Pir Vilayat left this life.

He had provided for the continued guidance of his students of the Sufi Path. Since 2000, his son, Pir Zia Inayat Khan, had been the acting spiritual leader of the Sufi Order International. In the interfaith tradition of his father and grandfather, Pir Zia has studied deeply and widely in the world's spritual wisdom, and has been trained in the classical Chistiyya mode and studied under the auspices of His Holiness the Dalai Lama. He is currently completing his doctoral studies in Religion at Duke University and, among his many other activities, has founded and acts as director of the Suluk Academy, an esoteric school located in upstate New York.

This is Pir Vilayat's tradition. Pir Vilayat wrote on the Sufi Order International Webpage regarding his work:

I am trying to develop an updated spirituality for our times. Following my father's message, I believe that to develop our being to its highest potential we need to discover our ideal and allow an inborn strength, a conviction in ourselves, to give us the courage toward developing this ideal. This requires both knowing our life purpose and mastery or discipline over ourselves in terms of body, mind, and emotions. With an attitude of joy and enthusiasm, we do not suppress but instead control and direct impulses toward the fulfillment of our goals. Instead of viewing life's setbacks as a hindrance, we can see them as an opportunity to discover and develop our creative power. As noted in all the religions, and most clearly evidenced in the life of Christ, we can transform suffering into joy. This means not denying suffering but rather accepting it, and thus gaining strength to be more masterful in life. At this time I believe we are called upon to give up resentments and prejudices, no matter how difficult that may be. Individual resentment hinders our unfoldment toward becoming our highest ideal; collective resentment causes wars. My deepest goal is to give those with whom I come into contact a respect and tolerance for each world religion, recognizing the unity of ideals behind the diversity of forms. I believe in rising above distinctions and differences to appreciate the beauty and variety in people and cultures and to uphold at all costs the dignity of every human being.

For twenty-seven years, almost every time Pir Vilayat Inayat Khan traveled from his home in France to the New York area, I heard him speak and attended his retreats. Sometimes I served as his chauffeur and aide. *The Sovereign Soul: Sufism: A Path for Today* is not an "official" text of the Sufi Order International. My book is not meant to proselytize or to try to convert. For me, Sufism and the teachings of Pir Vilayat have served as a point of departure, a touchstone guiding me in the exploration of my inner being. Each person who desires to find his or her own path will find it. This book describes mine.

Throughout *The Sovereign Soul* I often quote the writings of Pir Vilayat Inayat Khan. Sometimes I quote the writings of his father, referring to that Sufi master as Pir-o-Murshid Hazrat Inayat Khan. The word *pir* means "elder;" the title *murshid* is reserved by the Sufi order for those held in the highest esteem. The Sufis also employ the term "representative." A representative is someone whom a pir or a murshid appoints to represent that pir or murshid to students whom the teacher won't necessarily have time to attend to properly. The term *sheikh* is also used. A sheikh is roughly the equivalent of a pir or murshid. (Here the word "sheikh" has a specific spiritual connotation. I'm not referring to the many sheikhs who are active in the political world and about whom we read in the newspapers every day.) The terms pir, murshid, and sheikh are used somewhat interchangeably, particularly in the West. Generally, a pir or a sheikh is the leader of a Sufi order, of which there are many, or the head of a Sufi circle or a gathering of students within that order. These various definitions aren't rigid. Different Sufi orders have different hierarchical breakdowns.

My wife Majida and I are representatives. Majida's Christian name is Dawn, but, like members of most esoteric orders, she was given a "spiritual" name by her teacher to differentiate her greater self from her mundane personality. *Majida* means The Glorious One. I have a spiritual name too, *Musawwir*, which means "The Artist" or "The Fashioner." Majida and I are what might be termed as field workers in the spirituality business. For fifteen years we've run a small Sufi Order International Center from the spare bedroom of our apartment in Yonkers, New York. Just a few students, some of whom you'll meet later in this book, come to our center once a week to meet and share and meditate.   There are about one hundred and fifteen Sufi Order International centers in the U.S. today, many of them very small like ours.   There are somewhat more than two thousand Sufi Order International members in the U.S. as a whole, with perhaps an equivalent number in Europe and a few hundred in India and other countries.   There are also about a dozen other non-Sufi Order International orders in the U.S.

Majida and I, like the other Sufi Order International Center representatives, do our work quietly, with little fanfare.   Those who come for instruction and communion do so because they are compelled by an inner voice to be with others who share their need for personal growth and fulfillment.

What does that mean?   I will now tell you.

1

Happiness

I wander thro' each charter'd street,
Near where the charter'd Thames does flow,
And mark in every face I meet
Marks of weakness, marks of woe.
                    - WILLIAM BLAKE, *London*

The Angel that presided o'er my birth
Said, "Little creature, form'd of Joy & Mirth,
Go love without the help of any Thing on Earth."
                    - WILLIAM BLAKE, *Poems from Mss.*

The other night I was watching the movie *Ghost Busters II* for maybe the tenth time—you know, the one where ghosts and evil spirits wreak havoc on Manhattan. And as usual I had a good laugh at the mayor's line: "It's every New Yorker's God-given right to be just as miserable and unhappy as they want!"

Since I live in New York City, I can fully appreciate the comment. We New Yorkers even tend to take pride in this image. Maybe being miserable and unhappy would be lots of fun if only it didn't hurt so much. Living here in the city, I see, feel, experience and sometimes participate in deep unhappiness. I often experience the pain that a perfect stranger is feeling; I don't know what's causing it but I can feel its intensity. That experience is always hard on me. It gets me right in the gut, almost as if the pain were mine. And in a way it is. All of us are a single entity in the state the Sufis call *Wahdat Al-Wujud,* the Unity of Existence.

Unhappiness is universal. We all experience it and we all work at alleviating it. Or we get so used to it that it becomes our natural state and we get confused by moments of happiness and tend to reject them. Or we become addicted to the things we use to alleviate unhappiness—drugs and alcohol, for instance—and end up being unhappy on account of these addictions. Apparently, misery is all part of the human condition. Unhappiness is the rule—or so we think. The best thing we can say about unhappiness is that through experiencing it we come to understand what happiness is.

The Natural State of the Soul

What do we mean by happiness? As I explain later on, when we use a word in the mystical sense, which is what I'm doing here, we often mean something different from what the word ordinarily means. With this in mind, let's begin our discussion of happiness by saying what happiness is not. It is not pleasure, sexual, gastronomic, or intellectual. It is not euphoria, or ecstasy, although these feelings may be involved. It is not satisfaction (at a job well done, for instance), though again this may play a role.

The best definition I know of happiness, and one that Hazrat Inayat Khan used frequently, is that it is the natural state of the soul.

By the natural state of the soul, I mean that state of being in which we see all events and conditions as a part of the being of God.

Hazrat Inayat Khan writes:

> Earthly pleasures are the shadows of happiness because of their transitory character. True happiness is in love, which is the stream that springs from one's soul; and he who will allow this stream to run continually in all conditions of life, in all situations however difficult, will have happiness which truly belongs to him, the source of which is not without, but within. If there is a constant outpouring of love one becomes a divine fountain, for from the depth of the fountain rises the stream and, on its return, it pours upon the fountain, bathing it continually. It is a divine bath, the true bath in the Ganges, the sacred river. When once one has got the key of this fountain, one is always purified, every moment of one's life; nothing can stay in the mind causing man unhappiness! For happiness alone is natural, and it is attained by knowing and by living naturally.

If this is true—if happiness is the natural state of the soul—why is it so difficult to achieve? One reason is that we are usually in a poor state of communication with our soul. Usually, we don't even know that our soul exists. We tend to confuse personality with soul. The soul, though, is quite separate and different. We need to work hard at opening a channel to our soul. This is the path of meditation, of Sufism.

I have no idea why God made it so hard for us to be in touch with the soul. Certainly, being immured in the physical body doesn't help. Our physicality has persuaded our personality that we need to be bombarded by external stimuli in order to enjoy the worldly pleasures of which Hazrat Inayat Khan speaks. Our soul, however, knows that true happiness comes from within.

Let's suppose that we've been able to open a channel to the soul. Let's even suppose that we live in constant communion with our soul; that is quite possible. The problem, however, is that to the extent that we live in constant communion with our soul, we are never quite able to get very much done of value on the earth plane.

Cleaning house, for example, is out. (Guys tend to like this. "Sorry, honey, can't do the dishes right now, I'm communing.") Driving a car is definitely out. Talking to people is completely out unless the other person is in the same place as you are. In the state of deep meditation in which we are one with the soul, our personality has to step aside; it must not interfere. This is another one of those mysteries God has laid on us, but that's the way it is. A state of communion with the soul feels wonderful and is achievable, but it doesn't help us with the rent or the mortgage payments.

I'm not saying that going into deep meditation has no usefulness in the world. It is, after all, what we in the Sufi Order International are trained to do, and its value is incalculable. But as the depth of the reality that lies within is revealed to us, our reaction to the external world changes and there is a shift in the way our personality sees itself. There is always this problem, then: We have a soul whose natural state we aspire to experience and even to become.

We also have a personality that seeks to turn us away from this communion and back toward the outer world.

How do we reconcile soul and personality? As Hazrat Inayat Khan says, the key is to allow the love stream to flow. We must bring our feelings of resentment and guilt and inadequacy under control. It may be helpful to think of these feelings as valves or choke points you control even while you are vague about operating procedures. A good deal of spiritual discipline consists in locating these valves in ourselves and turning them to the proper positions. We have to remember the settings of the valves so we can go back and reset them whenever necessary. Finally, the valves dissolve, and the love stream flows unimpeded.

You can't achieve conscious control of the valves and choke points until you find out Who You Really Are as opposed to Who You Think You Are. Who You Think You Are—your image of yourself—is constructed from your actions during the day and the extent to which your actions serve your ego; it is molded by the directions your self-pity drives you in and it is defined by whether you are victim or victimizer, domineering or submissive, and by how much you expect from those around you.

The self-image that has been formed in us by our parents, by society and by religion, may not conform at all to who we really are. For example, if we think that we are quite loving when the truth is that we are actually very nasty, then we won't be able to neutralize our nastiness valve because we won't know that that nastiness valve is there to be neutralized. We must first of all take control of our self-image by recognizing what is true and what is false about that self-image. Only then can we adjust our valves and choke points so that the love stream can flow. We're so much bigger than the forces that made us who we think we are. In learning to access that bigness, we find out who we really are and become capable of adjusting the valves properly.

To be in balance is one attribute of happiness. How do you achieve that balance? By doing your meditations and your practices. By watching your breath.

You'll be amazed at how many questions I answer simply by saying do your practices; watch your breath. It isn't enough just to be a good person; if it were, everyone who was kind to dogs or children would be a mystic. The states described by Hazrat Inayat Khan and Pir Vilayat are interrelated. You could almost say that working on one of them is like working on all of them. (This isn't quite true, but it's true enough.) If you're doing the work, the happiness that is your birthright will come.

Hazrat Inayat Khan writes,

One does not take initiation for the sake of attaining happiness. It is true that one cannot attain wisdom without deriving a certain advantage from it, as it is more advantageous to be wise than ignorant. But it is not for this that the journey is entered upon. However, as he progresses on the spiritual path the Sufi becomes aware of a wonderful peace, which inevitably comes from the constant presence of God.

Many people of various beliefs and faiths have written about the practice of the presence of God, and all speak of the happiness they receive from being in His presence. So it is no wonder that the Sufi also, should he wish to speak of it, should testify to similar happiness. He does not claim to a greater happiness than his fellowmen, because he is a human being and subject to all the shortcomings of mankind. But at the same time others can decide about his happiness better even than his words can tell it. The happiness which is experienced in God has no equal in anything in the world, however precious that may be, and everyone who experiences it will realize the same.

You'll notice that Hazrat Inayat Khan says that we embark on the meditative journey to become wise and happiness is merely a byproduct of that journey. Hazrat Inayat Khan speaks of the sense of the presence of God that inevitably comes upon us when we advance along the path. When he speaks of this "constant presence of God," he means, I think, that we increasingly come to recognize that all things are a part of the being of God. This sounds nifty and is nice to think about—but it's also rather daunting, don't you think?

So you won't be intimidated by the prospect of coming more and more intimately into contact with ultimate reality as you pursue the path of meditation, I suggest that you start with smaller thoughts. As Hazrat Inayat Khan writes, "Happiness lies in thinking or doing that which one considers beautiful."

Now that's easier, don't you think? I'll give you an example of what I mean. A student once came to me who was very down on himself. I won't go into the details, but he thought that he was the very "pits"—the dregs of humanity. I gave him practices and meditations, but each time he came back he told me he hadn't been able to get into them.

After this had gone on for several months, I told him to go to a museum and look at the beautiful paintings, or to go to a zoo and enjoy the animals, or to seek out a natural setting and enjoy it. The suggestion worked. His condition improved. He'd needed to get used to the idea that beauty exists in the world.

If your mind has been focused on beauty, then when you are confronted with an ugly situation or an unpleasant person you have the means to deal with the ugliness. You can choose to remain in the serenity you've gained through the contemplation of beauty.

The Presence of God

Now we come to the tricky part. I'm not sure I'm even competent to talk about it. Reject what I say if you wish.

An awareness of the presence of God is not a given in our lives. Physical reality can seem to be quite "other than" and "outside of" the presence of God. Circumstances, whether internal or external, can virtually block out our experience of God's presence—even though all of reality is a part of that divine essence.

Being in the presence of God really means being a lens through which God looks at the physical universe. You have always possessed this quality of being a lens, but you may not have been aware of God's presence because, as a lens, your optical quality was not so good. Once you have become aware of God's presence and have acknowledged that presence in your life, then the awareness polishes the cloudy lens that is you. You know, even if only for a moment, that God is looking through your eyes. It is at this instant that the higher and lower aspects of your being meld into a single essence.

This is what I think Hazrat Inayat Khan is saying. The more we do the work of the spiritual school we've chosen, the better we become at refining and polishing the lens that is ourselves. As we do this work, an innocence grows within us that replaces the learned or assumed cynicism with which most of us face the world. Innocence is an essential component of our experiencing the natural state of the soul. That experiencing is happiness.

How do we achieve this state? We do our meditations! And we watch our breath.

You need to avoid performing what Pir Vilayat called a Spiritual Bypass Operation. Don't assume that you are in a state of spiritual advancement that you are not in and can't be in since you haven't done the work required to be in that advanced state. If, for example, you do a few spiritual exercises and then run around telling everyone how incredibly happy you feel, you've missed the point. You may even have a brief experience of the soul's sovereignty and begin to assume you've arrived. But you'll have to get comfortable with the fact that you're just beginning. Happiness actually depends on a certain level of spiritual maturity, on a calm knowledge of purpose and potential that you can access at will.

That in turn depends on the control of the breath. Hazrat Inayat Khan says:

As a horse can be controlled and directed by getting the reins in hand, so life can be controlled and directed by gaining control over breath. Every school of mystics has, as its most important and sacred teaching in the way of attainment, the control and understanding of the mystery of breath.

EXERCISE 1: *Balancing the Breath*

Here is a practice that is frequently given to newcomers. Though it is a beginning practice and may seem simple, it has the power to completely change your outlook, your attitude, and your being. The practice consists merely of counting while breathing. If you feel your pulse or your heart beat as you do this, so much the better. But it's not absolutely necessary to feel those things. What is necessary is the ability to maintain a regular beat as you count.

As you inhale, count to four. Then exhale and count to four. Inhale, four; exhale, four. That's it—except that you do it continually, every spare minute, until it becomes so automatic that you no longer think about it. Then you have balanced your breathing.

Though breathing practices can get elaborate, they all stem from this simple exercise. First you have to master the art of balanced breathing. If you've already done this, you can now move on to the next stage: practicing balanced breathing while you walk. As you walk, inhale four steps, then exhale four steps. Choose whatever pacing you find comfortable.

This is balance in action.

This is the kind of exercise I have in mind when I talk about watching the breath. Doing exercises like this is an essential component of spiritual attainment. The other essential component is doing those exercises religiously—no pun intended.

When I meet students from different paths (like Buddhism or Christian mysticism), I notice that, if they've been doing their exercises regularly for years, there is a certain affinity between us.

That affinity transcends any differences we may have in "theological" outlook. It almost doesn't seem to matter what discipline you follow as long as you actually follow it. You find the path you personally resonate to, and you follow that path.

It's a waste of time to swear allegiance to a teacher or discipline and then not follow through. When you don't follow through, all you do is swell the ranks of some organization and give yourself something to talk about at parties. Happiness is not attained by joining. Happiness is attained by doing.

Far too many of us have been so unhappy for so long that this state of being has become a familiar, comforting friend whom we are loathe to let go of. When, having seriously undertaken the pursuit of a spiritual path such as Sufism, we are all of a sudden confronted with the reality of what that spirituality is actually doing to our inner being, i.e., bringing it forth, empowering it—making us happy!—we can become terribly frightened.

"Oh, no!" we cry out blindly. "Not that!"

A response of this sort is, of course, a dead giveaway that we enjoy the state of being unhappy. After all, that state is one we are totally familiar with. We know all about it, it holds no uncomfortable surprises for us, and therefore we are most reluctant to part with it. Our state of unhappiness is fiendishly clever at thinking up reasons why we should not let go of it. We are often even proud of this state. After all, we invented it, and our state of unhappiness is for its part perfectly willing to accept the compromise we unconsciously offer it of looking like happiness on the surface. Beneath the surface, however, unhappiness still holds the reins; we are still looking at things in the old morbid ways.

The Importance of Community

It is because unhappiness is so persistent that being in a community of like-minded persons is so important. Imagine that, despite your penchant for clinging to unhappiness, you've managed to see some value in the spiritual order you've joined. You are determined that you will participate regularly in whatever the order has to offer you. Chances are that there will be others like yourself in attendance, others who will have a greater or lesser aptitude for coming to know their inner beings. Hopefully, the teachers themselves will be good at tapping into their own happiness, at allowing their own love stream to flow.

Seeing all this, you and your unhappiness can react in several ways. You can get annoyed. You can get angry at the teacher or at someone you perceive as being close to the teacher; you can vent your anger or you can let it seethe inside you. You can decide you don't like all this happiness flying around but that you will grit your teeth and bear it anyway, because you've taken a vow.

You can decide that you'll try to imitate those who seem better able to access their inner being than you, and that you'll stand next to them in class as much as possible. You can combine all the above and add a few wrinkles of your own. It doesn't matter all that much—except to you, of course—what the contents of your inner turmoil are, because you have truly decided that you will follow through regardless of the consequences.

Doing some or all of this will give you the opportunity to observe and absorb. That is the core of the student-teacher relationship: the student watches and copies and tries to imitate the teacher in all things. That's why so many students of spirituality seem to be clones of the teacher: they take this imitating to extremes. That isn't necessarily a bad thing. Students really do change at a deep level, even though an observer may regard changes like those of speech and dress as superficial. Authentic change occurs within because the student is also observing and imitating important things, such as the way the teacher relates to the outside world and the way the teacher connects with the source of inner peace.

Another reason for being regularly in the presence of the teacher and of more advanced students is simply to absorb, on an unconscious level, the energy around you. If you hang out with such people long enough, you'll begin to be affected by what they do and how they feel. Naturally, you can reject the energy you seem to be absorbing and continue to feel miserable. I've seen many people do that. They need to be around people who have a degree of spiritual contentment, but they are so invested in their own unhappiness that they simply refuse to go the next step of allowing the absorption process to proceed. These are the people who flit around the peripheries of spiritual groups pretending to be committed while never actually making the commitment, promising they will take the next step but never actually doing so. I think that often these people have been so damaged by their lives that they simply cannot imagine feeling whole; such a concept is beyond their ken. If that's the case with you, perhaps seeing a good therapist is in order. It's not that you can't break through; it's just that you may need a lot of help to do so. The presence of a teacher may not be enough.

If you allow yourself to be fully in the presence of those further along the path—the advanced students and the teacher—and permit their energy to permeate you, you'll discover that this kind of exposure helps you to change. If you hang out with happy people long enough, you'll become happy too. It's like playing chess with good chess players; you may never be as good as they are but you'll certainly be better than you were before.

Asking God to change you has a profound effect. I remember once when one of my students told me that something I'd said had affected her profoundly; she had even written it down and taped it to her computer. This stroked my ego nicely, even though I couldn't recall saying what she said I'd said. I responded by declaring: "When you ask the question, the asking changes you." What I meant is that you will change if you ask God what to do. If you ask Him how you can experience happiness, that changes you. If you simply ask Him to create the conditions within your being that will allow the love stream to flow, that changes you too.

There are many reasons why prayer is so extraordinarily powerful, but the main one is that in the act of prayer you allow yourself to become a supplicant. It might be said that those who truly desire the love stream to flow within and who have been willing to submit the personality to the required modifications, have put themselves in a powerful position. They've acknowledged the possibility that happiness exists and that they can experience it. They've sent the message that they are willing to learn how to experience happiness.

Can you see the power in this attitude?

Stop reading for a moment and think about your access to the inner stream of love. Allow yourself to know what is real, to go beyond your feelings of guilt and inadequacy and just know what is real. Now, think of how you might formulate a question to God—a supplication, a plea, a simple statement of what you're looking for. Then ask the question, and see what happens. The answer may take a while in coming, but God always answers. Just be patient—and remember to follow through on that vow you made to God.

2

Commitment

The initiate takes a vow in his heart to make use to the best of
his ability of all he receives from the Sufi teaching and practices,
not using any parts for selfish purposes.
                          - HAZRAT INAYAT KHAN

Once I'd been initiated, I found myself in that
Never-never-land where you know you've done
something significant with your life but you're not
sure what.

I still thought of myself as a hippie, living on the edge,
never taking society too seriously. When I mention this to
my younger students now they laugh, but we took being a
hippie very seriously back in the 1970s. What was my life
like then? I had a room in a boarding house with a shared
kitchen where I fixed my meals. I worked as a carpenter
for a small construction firm. I drove a rusty black 1965
Nova that burned up barrels of oil half of which I left
behind on the road. I went out with a girl friend from
England who was very sweet and who took me to my first

Pir Vilayat seminar, for which I am eternally grateful, and if I knew where she was I would thank her.

Since I was living in Boston, I started taking classes at the Sufi Order International Center. Soon I was deep into basic Sufism. This was in July 1979. At that time the Order had a community house called the Khanaqa as-Safiya, on Fourteenth Street in New York City. (*Khanaqa,* or *Khanqah,* is a Farsi word meaning a house or an abode of sufis and dervishes.) I was asked to come down and live at the Khanaqa as-Safiya to help prepare for a three-day symposium that Pir Vilayat was hosting.

It was while I was living at the Khanaqa that I met the love of my life. Back in my former pre-Sufi existence, I'd had a vision one day—a vision of a woman. It was a strange sort of vision, because the woman hardly seemed real at all. It was as if I had experienced the soul of this woman, her essence. I felt there couldn't possibly be anyone like her for me, that it had to be my imagination. Besides, I was married. I dismissed this vision as a self-generated fantasy, rationalized it as the yearning we all have for the idealized Beloved. But I didn't forget it.

As it turned out, the person of my dreams was living at the Khanaqa. I didn't recognize her at first. This was because I was busy digesting the fact that the majority of those involved in spiritual matters at the Khanaqa—I would say seventy-five percent—were women; they also made up the majority of the residents. The unexpected presence of all these women taking an intense interest in spirituality initially distracted me from noticing that the woman of my dreams was at the Khanaqa. Also interfering was my emotional state: I had just gotten over a wife, and I was still getting over a girl friend. But nevertheless, Majida, the woman of my vision, was indisputably there. She'd had a vision of a man in the same way I'd had a vision of a woman—and that man was me. For a while we circled each other warily, our mutual reaction being, "Oh my God, what do I do about this?" Finally we got together. Today we are married and co-directors of a Sufi center.

So there were a number of factors that were causing perturbations in my psyche: the Khanaqa as-Safiya, all that I was learning about Sufism, the abundant presence there of spiritually-minded women—and the presence of Majida. That wasn't all. There was also New York City. I found this urbane metropolis hugely intimidating. I'm a country boy, raised in Minnesota, and I had lived in rural settings most of my life. Now I was in New York City, and I had no city moves. I also had vocabulary problems, self-aware-ness problems and money problems—and I tended to be morose and wallow in self-pity (or so I was told, more than once, in fact many times). So I had all this to contend with and I was truly rattled. But I also had a job I'd agreed to do, and I was determined to do it.

That job was to be a Sufi. You see (as I've already explained), I'd taken a vow.

I had all the hang-ups listed above, plus a few more I won't mention, but through it all I was aware that I had taken a vow—two vows, in fact. One was to the Sufi Order International. The other was to Pir Vilayat person-ally. There was no way I wasn't going to follow through on this two-fold vow.

We find it easy to make a commitment these days. We know that we don't really have to mean it. At any time, we can decide not to follow through. We can decide that it was all a mistake in the first place.

Maybe we're lax about commitment because we're so used to being fooled. We've been lied to so often by the society we live in—by our government, by our religious leaders, by our teachers, by the media, sometimes by our own families—that we don't know who to believe anymore. If you can't believe anybody, you can easily reverse any decision you make simply by saying: "They lied to me."

That's an acceptable excuse these days. We hear it all around us, and we see it backed up by the uninterrupted parade of Hollywood conspiracy theory movies that appear on TV and parade through our movie theatres. For some years after I joined the Sufi Order International, even I still struggled with the belief that spirituality is some sort of scam. The struggle got particularly intense whenever I was on the verge of making a breakthrough in my practices. There was always a part of me that wondered if it weren't all just a hustle.

But sometimes the commitment we make is the right one. Seeing its rightness may be difficult because we have to throw off so many years of social conditioning. It can be all the more difficult to see when we try to make a commitment to something that society regards as marginal. That was my situation: I was battling against all the societal conditioning that considers Sufism, and so much else that is valuable, to be marginal and possibly a scam.

But in a way I wasn't struggling at all. For it hadn't been the strange far-out ideas of the order that had attracted me to Sufism. It had been the light of my teacher. What Pir Vilayat was saying, the vibrations he gave forth, all seemed to me to have the authentic ring of truth. Ultimately, what drew me into his presence day after day was the way he said things I found I could believe—that, and a voice inside me that kept saying, "This is your teacher."

To put it another way: Before I met Pir Vilayat, I'd already begun to ponder in my limited way the ideas he seemed to embody, and I needed him to complete what I'd begun within myself in my own halting manner.

For conventional society, Bhagwan Shree Rajneesh has become the symbol of why gurus are dangerous. The ninety-three Rolls-Royces he owned spring to mind whenever gurus are mentioned. They're like a Scarlet Letter proclaiming what's untrustworthy in a spiritual leader.

But whenever Pir Vilayat visited us there wasn't a luxury car to be seen. I'd come to the center with an enormous number of ingrained prejudices about gurus. But I couldn't see that Pir Vilayat had any qualities remotely similar to those that the stereotyped, societally-stigmatized, guru is supposed to have. Second, it wouldn't have mattered if he did. The preconceptions taught me by society, my ideas about what a center would be like—all of that faded away once I'd decided that Pir Vilayat was my man. Then I readily took my vow.

The Life-Time Vow

The vow is for life. It has to be. How can you find out if what you've dedicated yourself to works if you regard it as a stop-gap measure, something you're doing until something better comes along? Let me illustrate with a story that Hazmat Inayat Khan tells in *The Alchemy of Happiness*:

In a village there was once a young peasant who was known to be a great seeker after truth. A great teacher came to that village, and it was announced that for whoever came into the presence of this teacher, the doors of heaven would be opened, and he would be admitted without having to account for his deeds. The peasants were very excited about this, and they all went to the teacher except this young man. The teacher said, "Everyone from the village came to me except that young man. I shall go to him myself." So he went to the cottage of this young man and said, "What is it? Is it that you are antagonistic to me, or that you doubt my knowledge? What is it that has kept you from coming to see me?" And he said, "There was nothing that kept me back except this one thing: I heard the announcement that everyone in your presence would be admitted to heaven without question. And I do not seek this admission, because although I had a teacher once I do not know where he is, in heaven or in hell. If I went to heaven and he was in the other place it would be terrible for me! Heaven would become hell for me. I would rather be with my teacher wherever he is."

Obviously there's a limit. You have to be wary of the real wackos, like the ones who release poison gas in the subways of Tokyo or the ones who insist that only white people have rights because—well, who knows why, but I'm sure they think their reasons are good ones.

When you make a real commitment, it's something that only you know about. You can't tell anybody about it who doesn't have it; it will make no sense to that person. Somebody who does have it will simply say, "Well, of course." Real commitment is something you either have or don't have. It seems to be a function of who you are, and it's something that can't be forced.

If you're worried because you can't commit yourself to anything, maybe it's because nothing has come along so far that really inspires you. On the other hand, if you're good at commitment, if you are already committed to your family or your profession or to an avocation that you genuinely love, then the step on to a spiritual commitment will potentially be easy for you.

All you have to do is decide how far you want to push the envelope of your beliefs. What I mean by this is that when you commit yourself spiritually, your personality doesn't completely understand what you're doing. In committing yourself, you may be quite happily prepared to drop the concept of God that was inculcated in you as a child in favor of what you are sure is the deeper divinity of the God you're committing yourself to in the spiritual group.

But, even if you have no trouble dropping the God of your childhood, your personality will demand that you begin the journey along the path with at least some concept of God. It will demand that you invent a new God image. And, almost inevitably, for its own comfort, your personality will give your "new God" some of the trappings of the concept that you thought you had left behind.

Towards a New God

Perhaps you'll invent a God of retribution; perhaps you'll invent a God of compassion; perhaps you'll invent a God of love. All these are fine inventions. The trouble is, none of your inventions will resemble the God of Sufism.

According to Ibn 'Arabi, the names of God are infinite, but He has ninety-nine names that are attributes mentioned in the Quran. These are the source of the names. Some of these qualities (and the associated names) seem negative to Westerners. For example, one of them is *Al-Darr*, "He Who Distresses." Another is *Al-Khafid*, "He Who Abases." (He who distresses and abases you!)

You and I would probably prefer a God who is exclusively compassionate, one who wouldn't hurt a kitten let alone cause a human being distress. In our culture we tend to have difficulty with a God who watches with an air of amused tolerance over a universe of interactions of physical/emotional/spiritual energy.

God's nature is unknown—that is, unknown, for the time being, to you. In light of that, you may want to make things easier for yourself by focusing your commitment a bit. State just what you want from this commitment. Is it personal transformation? Is it world peace?

My own favorite desire is to die consciously. I'm training myself to be able to make a conscious transition from this world to the next. I don't like the idea of going fearfully into the night, of slipping into the next level of existence—whatever its nature may be—in a state of paralysis. Part of the reason I work so hard on meditation and spirituality is so that when the moment of death comes, I can be awake enough to enjoy the whole thing. I badly want to attain this goal of dying consciously. Concentrating on that goal helps me overcome the momentary tremors I feel as I advance along the spiritual path. After all, although the path is ever unfolding to further knowledge, it is ever unknown as well.

Hazrat Inayat Khan says,

It is the ideal which prompts man to sacrifice, and the most important thing he can sacrifice is his own life. A man without ideal has no depth; he is shallow. However pleased he may be with his every-day life, he can never enjoy that happiness which is independent of outer circumstances. The pleasure which is experienced through pain is the pleasure experienced by the idealist. But what of the pleasure that has not come out of pain? It is tasteless. Life's gain, which people think so much of, what is it after all? A loss caused by an ideal is a greater gain than any other gain in this world. You must find your ideal in yourself; no ideal in life will prove lasting and true except the one you yourself make.

Another way of pushing the envelope consists in look-ing at yourself and gauging the extent of the depths within you. Many people seem shallow, and many people ARE shallow—but that's only because they haven't yet accessed their own inner depths. In making a commitment to medi-tation and spirituality, you have to decide how deep you will dare to be. You have to decide how mighty the goals you set yourself will be. In this universe, everything is pos-sible. As Hazrat Inayat Khan says, you must create the most profound ideal you can, an ideal which, although it will ultimately give pleasure, is born of pain.

EXERCISE 2: *Imagining the Master*

Get into a space that is as quiet as it can be.

Balance your breath; breathe in and out evenly and regularly. Note that, as you do so, your breath automatically slows down. It will take a little work to learn how to do this; do not be discouraged if slowing the breath seems elusive.

When you feel relaxed enough, turn your attention to a master or a saint or a great being whom you admire. See if you can identify what it is about that being that you find so appealing. Is it something that history tells us this person did? Is it something about this person's essence that you imagine to be true? Do you feel a connection between you and this person, as if the closeness originates from her or him and not only from you? Whatever it is, and it could be a combination of things, see if you can find these attributes in yourself.

There is a slight variant on this exercise which consists in your trying to imagine that you are authentic, whole, and capable. You do this by choosing a living teacher—a guru, sheikh, or other spiritually accomplished person with whom you are familiar—and then imagining what it's like to be that person. Remember that such persons are human after all, and that they have their own quirks. Imagine that they exude a certain awareness that is both charming and compelling. Imagine how the great being experiences her or his own energy. Imagine that you possess a similar energy. Imagine that, although you remain "yourself," you share some aspect of that being's spirituality.

The idea behind this exercise is that you cannot identify a quality in somebody else unless you have that quality within yourself. Ordinarily this idea is used to show us that we have the same capacity for foibles and sin as someone else, but it can also be used to demonstrate that we are great beings. What you are doing here is discovering an ideal self within you and dedicating yourself to the unfolding of this self. You'll have to push the envelope of your concept of yourself very hard to include this new discovery; and you'll have to push it even harder to accommodate the new sense of being that will make it a reality.

Note that the part of you that is reading this book and judging whether or not you measure up to the above is your personality, your surface sense of yourself. True com-

mitment comes from deep within ourselves. The surface
sense of self must give way to this; it must table its criti-
cisms and judgments and adjust its attitudes and perceptions to finally allow this deeper self to hold sway.

Assuming that the personality is willing! If you notice a
massive amount of unwillingness in yourself, it may mean
that the time hasn't come yet for you to make a commitment. It may also mean finally that, as good as it looked at
the time, this is not really the kind of commitment that is
appropriate for you. It may be that not only your personality but your inner self as well, is resisting. If this is happening, your inner self may have cause.

Examine your situation carefully. Other reasons for resistance may be terror, or fear of the unknown, or fear of
change—or all of the above. This is where the reassur-
ances of a spiritual peer group and a spiritual guide are
particularly valuable; their presence means you are not conducting your spiritual journey in a vacuum. No one in the
group will force you or cajole you into doing something
you don't want; this simply isn't done.

The Non-Being of Separateness

The older I get, the more aware I become of how isolated we human beings feel ourselves to be no matter what
our circumstances. Those drawn to the spiritual life feel
this especially. It is likely because they have been treated as
a little odd most of their lives. It is only fairly recently that
I have had the experience of directly realizing how precious is our coming together in Sufism. It was when I was
at a representatives' camp that I suddenly saw all of the

people there, whom I had known for years, as the most beloved of my friends, and saw how amazingly important this was to me. Up to that point, I'd been so involved in my own psycho/spiritual meanderings that I hadn't really noticed anyone else. I now realize that it was an initiation of sorts, my feeling what I felt: that those around me were my most precious family, that they were as much a part of my own growth and even of myself as they were a part of their own growth and of themselves—that we were all aspects of the One Being. Unfortunately, we humans have the habit of feeling isolated; probably we are taught to feel this way. But it is a mistaken feeling.

Commitment can be seen as the allowing of beauty to enter our lives, as the allowing of the desire for intimate spiritual expression to come forward and become itself— as the acknowledgement of our capacity for evoking the divine being within ourselves.

I recommend now that you put this book down, slow your breath down in the way I've indicated above, and turn your attention to who you would like to become if you could become who you are. See if you can find the kernel of purity within yourself that is the truth of your essence; then, water it and fertilize it.

This is true commitment: nurturing within yourself the kernel of truth and purity that is what you already are.

3

Personal Problems

Through every condition, agreeable or disagreeable, the soul
makes its way towards the goal. - HAZRAT INAYAT KHAN

There is a story about Saint Theresa of Avila, the
Spanish visionary nun who lived from 1515 to 1582.
She was on the road, traveling by coach to answer
questions before the Inquisition. It was night; it was rain-
ing; it was muddy, and the coach ran off the road into a
ditch. As she extricated herself from the vehicle, Saint
Theresa heard a voice declaiming from the sky: "Dost thou
not know, Theresa, that this is how I treat my friends?"

The exhausted saint, her vision blurred by raindrops,
looked up into the night sky and shrieked, "Is it small wonder, then, that Thou hast so few of them?"

There's no reason to suppose your life is going to get
easier just because you've begun to meditate. You may
expect this to happen because one of the come-ons for

meditation classes is stress reduction. Meditation has this effect, I suppose, but "stress reduction meditation" is not meditation. It's a series of breathing and relaxation exercises you have to perform before you can move on to meditation.

But such exercises are really just a bare beginning. Pir Vilayat used to chuckle at the whole idea of meditation as a calming technique, declaring that this constituted a very superficial approach. He was very clear in saying that you have to have a better reason for meditating, because once you begin to meditate in earnest, your problems will multiply.

Personal problems come in all shapes and sizes and levels of intensity. Some are as a simple as having a splinter in your finger. Others are more complex and serious, like being a war refugee. Nevertheless, most personal problems fall into the "I'm not happy" category. Look at your current personal problems and see if they don't all really fall under that heading.

We tend to see our personal problems as external in origin rather than generated by ourselves. And, certainly, some of our problems are external in origin: becoming a war refugee is hardly a self-generated state and belongs in the accident category; it's a case of being in the wrong place at the wrong time (besides, war is a category unto itself, and it's one I don't want to deal with in this book).

In many cases, our personal problems are such that we should almost consider them a luxury item in the light of many of the problems that bedevil the world today. To have a good reason for saying, "I'm not happy," is a whole lot better than having a good reason for saying, for example, "I'm starving, and soldiers conscripted my 12-year-old boy into the army last week."

If you do have the luxury of personal problems, it would be a sin for you to waste this opportunity God that has given you. It would be a mistake for you to think that because people are in distress in Somalia your personal problems do not have significance. God goes to a great deal of trouble to ensure that there are people in the world who have the luxury of personal problems—and besides, you're not in Somalia.

Moreover, it is a mistake to think that in our world of *Maya* (the Sanskrit word for *illusion*) we should train ourselves not to be affected by a problem unless it's so huge we are forced to pay attention. That's silly. It may be Maya, it may be illusion—but if you break your arm, I guarantee you that the illusion is going to hurt. It is the same with emotional distress—illusion or not, it hurts.

Personal Problems and Our Innermost Potential

If we let them, personal problems can activate our innermost potential. Most people come to a compromise agreement with what they think their lives are about. The agreement may be wholly out-of-synch with what is real, but by its nature it is a comfortable one—we have come up with it in the first place in order to be comfortable—and usually we've framed it in such a way that those around us, having created their own compromise agreements, have no trouble going along with ours.

Once we start meditating, we violate our compromise agreement—which was bogus anyway—and begin to feel uncomfortable. At one point, I had a self-pity problem I did not own up to. I created other problems for myself because of my blindness to this problem. Finally acknowledging the problem, however, didn't mean it went away. It stayed around—but it got re-filed in my embarrassment drawer, so that now when it comes up I have the presence of mind to get embarrassed rather than indulge in a self-pity wallow.

It's helpful to see your problem from as many different angles as possible. If you can detach your point of view, even if just a little, even if just for a moment, from your personality, and look at that problem as if it belonged to a friend and wasn't your own at all, then you might be able to discover aspects of the problem that you hadn't noticed when you were so intimately wrapped up in it. If the problem involves two people (don't they always?), perhaps it will help to see yourself and the other person as players interacting on a stage. Better still, try getting into the consciousness of the other person, becoming that person for a time, seeing things from his or her point of view (which point of view, however wholly mistaken you know it to be, that other person persists in clinging to for some strange reason). If you can do this—if only for a moment—then your whole take on the relationship might change.

Once you've shifted perspective, even if only slightly, you're ready for step two: Finding the cause within the cause. In the case of my self-pity problem, the causes within the causes were, in descending order: a feeling of ineffectiveness; a feeling of inadequacy; a need for attention; confusion about my purpose in life—and, beneath all this, the knowledge that my purpose in life was one of service. What had started out deep in my psyche as a need to serve had become, by the time it worked its way to the surface of my consciousness, a feeling of self-pity.

All of this takes work. The key is to admit that maybe your way of seeing things is a touch skewed from the vision of things you came into this world with, that it is a bit distorted from your original desire. What was that original desire? Why, it was the vow you took, before you were born, to fulfill your part of God's great plan. It was the thrust of evolution propelling you forward. It was whatever you think it was, as long as that thought is at the outermost edge of what you can conceive.

The Problem Was Always Yours

A note of caution: While it's true that our original desires survive the transition into incarnation on this planet, still, as our body grows and our personality develops, pollution, or more accurately intoxication, enters the picture. The genetic inheritance from our parents, the environment we're reared in—both serve to modify and distort the purity of our pre-life eternity desires. That's how it is. Beats me why God set things up in this way, but He did.

It does absolutely no good to get into a parent-blaming mode. The problem is yours now. You own it. And while bashing your parents or other relatives (and as a last resort God) may give you a certain temporary satisfaction, it is pointless. Going to them and saying, "You really screwed this up in me; now fix it," will not work

If you're going to travel the path of the mystic, understand that certain things must be left behind. You may find that when you're with your family you have to pretend that nothing within you has changed. You do this simply because to do otherwise would be too upsetting for them. Most of my acquaintances on the path tell me their parents know they're into something odd but never ask about it. Once my mother came to visit me for a few days, saying she would leave on Sunday night. When she discovered I was performing the worship service that Sunday and more or less expected her to attend, she found an excuse for leaving Sunday morning. At the time, this really upset me, but I came to understand that within her world she could do nothing else. To admit I was doing what was so strange to her would have rattled her reality entirely too much. And so she left on Sunday morning.

Hazrat Inayat Khan writes, "The Message is a call to those whose hour has come to awaken, and it is a lullaby to those who are still meant to sleep."

Pir-o-Murshid also says that it is a sin to awaken a sleeper. And so it is. Besides, you usually won't succeed, and will end up with a hysterical person on your hands. Remember, a lot of what happens on the spiritual path is scary for the personality that hasn't been prepared by a hierarchy of teachers to handle it. It's even scary for the personality that *has* been prepared!

EXERCISE 3: Shahid: *The Witness*

Here's an exercise you can do every day, one that will help you immensely in sorting out the causes of your problems. When you go to bed and enter into the state of reverie known as the alpha state, that comes just before sleep, review your entire day. Backwards or

forwards, it doesn't matter which, but pick one and stick to it; other-
wise your subconscious will get confused, and we don't want confusion
at this stage.

The key is to look at the events of the day without judging your
actions or the actions of others. Just look. In Sufism, we call this
exercise Shahid—*The Witness. Shahid is completely neutral in*
attitude. There is no judgment.

The results of this exercise depend on how good you get at it. As
in anything else, you have to work at it, and the harder you work at
it the sharper your perceptions become. The description I've just
given is essentially it; no further elaboration is necessary.

Michael

I had a friend named Michael who, if he was not my best friend, was among the top two or three. In 2002, Michael's doctors told him he had type four cancer of the stomach and only had three weeks left to live. It was as if they were thinking, "He's a goner. Now, who's next on our list?"

Worse still, Michael agreed. At different times we told him he had a choice: He could give up or he could fight.

Six months later, Michael's prognosis was, if not wonderful, at least stable. Better yet, Michael's attitude was improving and his being was expanding, both visibly.

I was happy things were improving for Michael and I visited him as often as I could, to cheer him on and because of the great conversations we were having. I couldn't help feeling, though, that on an unconscious level at least some of our friends were disappointed by Michael's continued survival. They were believers in that strange school of psychology that says that Michael was responsible for his own illness; that he was somehow making himself into a martyr, suffering and dying for the sins of the rest of us; or that his illness was his wife Sharifa's fault, since a few years before she had insisted they stay in New York even though Michael's guide had advised him to move out on account of the stress of big-city living, and so on.

I'm ashamed to say that I bought into some of this. I came to my senses when one of the group told me that he'd been glad to hear I'd shed tears for Michael. What the hell was this person thinking, I wondered? That because I'd bought into these "reasons" for Michael's illness, I couldn't weep for my friend? That's when I realized that Michael was sick—period. That was all there was to it. No undercurrents of gloom or doom had created his condition. People get sick because sickness is a part of life.

At the same time I realized how myopic our view of life can get. What happened was that our little group of Sufis, of which Michael and I were members, had gone into a panic. There are only twenty to thirty of us in the group at any one time, and this was the first time that any one of us had gotten seriously ill. We'd had a couple of accidental deaths but no life-threatening diseases, and now, thrown off balance by Michael's illness, we were desperately searching for an answer. We *had* to understand—even if it meant assigning two-thirds of the blame to Michael and/or his wife and one-third to ourselves. Somehow, somewhere, we had to find fault.

It seems that the further removed we are from a critical situation, the more likely we are to assign blame. If we're really close to somebody who's sick, we just want that person to get well. But the further outside the intimate circle we are, the more likely we are to simply become impatient. All of which might lead you to believe that our personal problems loom very large for us while the problems of others are important only to the extent that our ego is bound up with them.

That's the way it is. This is just another example of how God set things up. If you've got a splinter in your finger, all you can think about is getting it out. If the splinter is in someone else's finger, that's that person's problem. You may offer helpful advice, such as, "I have tweezers specifically designed for splinter removal, which I will gladly loan you," but you'll probably add, "As for extracting the splinter, that's up to you." This is not very different from the way in which spiritual guides, including myself, regard the personal problems people bring to us, with the one addition (besides the compassion we feel) that we tend to look at those problems with an eye to seeing what new qualities of soul are forcing their way through the morass of personality to cause these difficulties.

The first step in dealing with your problems is to work on seeing how many of them are self-generated. Here's where the practice of reviewing each day comes in handy. You need to review your whole life, watching it as if it were a movie and trying to find places where you made a decision that could have gone any number of ways, but you chose that particular way.

Truth is basic to this practice. You have to learn to look at your life unwaveringly, without excuses. And, however tempting it may be, you have to be very careful about turning the light of truth on other people. We seem to feel that when we find something out about ourselves that is true but unpleasant, we are under an obligation to point that unpleasant quality out to everyone else who possesses it. Don't do that. Saying "I always tell the truth" is just an excuse for hurting other people. Sufism holds that, given the unknowable nature of the universe, telling the truth is impossible, since we can never know the whole of a thing or even begin to suspect all of its ramifications. So, restrict truth-telling to self-examination.

And avoid beating up on yourself. There is this idea, left over from the Middle Ages, that self-flagellation is a necessary adjunct to the pursuit of the mystical life or for that matter of any kind of religious or spiritual experience. This is silly. The goal is not self-recrimination but rather discovering the qualities that are asserting themselves in your being. You'll have no trouble knowing what your deficiencies are, because as soon as you start the process of self-examination they will show up.

What a spiritual guide wants for you is that at the same time as you are discovering your many flaws, you learn about your own splendor. We desire for you to remember that your being is a part of the being of God and that God desires to get it right, whatever "right" may be. The only way God can get it right is through the process of your own self-realization.

Pir Vilayat spoke of an inverted pyramid relationship with God, one where a sea of energy narrows down to us mortals who are at the (inverted) apex of the pyramid and are the real focus of the energy, which energy of necessity restricts itself to our limited incarnate beings. The more we can surmount our self-pity and the opinions of others about ourselves and our relationship to reality, the more we are able to acquire a conscious realized knowledge of the degree to which we are involved in this pyramidal relationship with God.

I have already quoted Ibn 'Arabi as saying that the Names of God and of His Attributes and Qualities are limitless. You can get some idea of the possibilities by reading the list of Ninety-Nine Names of God as they are known to Islam. If your text lists the Ninety-Nine Names with lengthy explanations for each one, ignore the explanations and simply contemplate the literal English translation. Explanations are always opinions; develop your own explanations.

The Role of the Teacher

Teachers serve this useful purpose, that as students we are able to measure ourselves against our teachers, not competitively, but comparatively. I'll be dealing with the guide/teacher/student relationship periodically throughout this book, so for now I'll simply say that this kind of a measuring rod can be very useful. And when you're in the group that surrounds your teacher, you can measure yourself against those of your peers who have gained your respect. Of course, you can only measure yourself against your teacher or the individuals you admire in your group if you're capable of making rational judgments about what you are looking at.

The best thing for some people is simply to be told, "Here, work on this." At the time, the instruction might not make sense to the student, but if it comes from someone whose intuition the student trusts (hopefully, his or her guide), then that student can simply go along with it and ignore other considerations. For others, it's necessary to be a little more circumspect. The former tends to be my approach as a teacher—though, to tell the truth, I'm not sure how much I tend to rely on somebody else's word myself, even my own guide's word, if that word isn't matched by some sort of intuitive corroboration in myself. So ultimately the responsibility lies with the student to decide whether or not to accept a given instruction.

I really don't concern myself with my own personality all that much because I've discovered a unit of measurement within that sums it all up. It is this: I used to be really a jerk, and now I'm less of one. My jerkhood has decreased as my faith in my inner being has increased. How do I know? Because Majida says so. Trust me when I tell you never to argue with my wife.

(I should add that I know students who are able to dissect their personalities with accuracy and objectivity. If you're in that group, continue to do so. Don't let anything I say deflect you from doing what you feel is right for yourself.)

To return to my friend Michael: I don't think his cancer was the external manifestation of an emerging quality or qualities. I think he got sick, and that sickness is a part of the human condition that we all must face to a greater or lesser degree. There's no doubt that the manner in which Michael made his decisions while suffering from the disease reflected emerging qualities. And, in his case, he was able to provide those around with him with a series of excellent lessons in how to inwardly react positively to severe external circumstances.

Finally, try to remember from time to time that you are a Being of Lght. This is a key concept in Sufism, one that cannot be described but can only be experienced. Our light-beingness is bigger, much bigger, than any personal problem that can possibly come along and annoy our physical vehicle—bigger, in fact, than the entire physical universe.

Whatever made you think you were smaller than your problems?

Think bigger. Much bigger!

4

The Path of Embarrassment

He who thinks himself wise, O heaven, is a great fool. - VOLTAIRE

Sufism is called the path of the heart and the path of power. It is also called the path of blame and the path of poverty. It is all these and more. I like to call it the path of embarrassment. Whatever your spiritual path, initially embarrassment plays a role.

Nobody likes to be embarrassed (except those who get paid for it); generally, we make every effort to avoid embarrassment. We don't mind watching other people being embarrassed; that's why we watch sitcoms. (Frankly, I never met a sitcom I liked. But that's just me. Maybe you think they're great.) The fact is that we enjoy being entertained by embarrassing situations, though we'd rather avoid being in embarrassing situations ourselves.

However, that isn't quite what I'm talking about.

I'm talking about the moment when you look at yourself and are greatly embarrassed to discover that you're a jerk, that you're confused and uncaring and morally ambivalent, that you can't keep a coherent thought in your head, that you're completely full of yourself, that you're totally steeped in self-pity—pick any or all of the above or make up your own list. I'm talking about the moment when you suddenly discover that possibly, just possibly, you have something to learn about being a human being.

That moment of discovery isn't fun.

Sufism holds that pathways begin to form in our brain from the moment of birth. These pathways deepen and send out branches and take on different colorations as we grow older. They are our habits of thought, which evolve as our notions about ourselves and our place in the universe evolve. Often the habits of thought we have as adults are the result of decisions we make very early on in our lives, even when we're toddlers.

Most of us never try to change these pathways. As we grow older we continue to support the decisions we made as toddlers. We never try to reassess these decisions in the light of maturity.

Yet it's our job, once we have become aware of those pathways, to consciously direct or redirect their growth and change their coloration. To do this we must identify the contents of each pathway, and identifying those contents can cause us a great deal of self-embarrassment. It's very hard to rise above this embarrassment. These lines appear in the writings of the Swedish film director Ingmar Bergman:

> The aerialist said to the actor, "My job is very dangerous. Every night I risk my life."
> The actor replied to the aerialist, "That's nothing. Every night I risk my ego."

Your Own Truth

In the preceding chapter we looked at personal problems. We examined the causes of these problems in order to try to discover how the energy contained in them might be redirected in more positive directions.

When you've identified a problem's cause, what you have on your hands is an embarrassment. When you've reflected on this embarrassing quality you quickly become aware of how interwoven it is with many other parts of your life.

People sometimes come to me in great distress—I'm frequently in that state myself—because they've just discovered some new, disturbing, and very embarrassing truth about themselves. They've found out they're selfish. They've discovered that feelings of contempt play a big part in their lives. They've realized that they are often critical of others for no good reason. They've discovered that they treat their wife, their husband, their children, their dog, their cat, their goldfish—and others—badly.

It makes them very unhappy to see these things in themselves.

I tell them three things:
• The purer we become, the more aware we become of the flaws we had and still have. The holiest of monks knows he is the worst of sinners.
• The fact that you are seeing these qualities at all means that the work you are doing on yourself has been effective.
• We may have just noticed a flaw, but that doesn't mean the flaw is new. It may always have been there, but we're just now noticing it. This noticing means that we are now able to deal with it.

Frustrating, isn't it? You take up meditation expecting to hear celestial choirs singing and see fireworks going off, and what you get is, "I'm a jerk." Maybe at the start you heard an angel singing and saw fireworks exploding—that often happens initially—but inevitably, if you do the work, what comes up is, "I'm a jerk."

At this point you need to remember how to breathe. Nothing fancy; just pay attention to your breathing. You'll notice that just giving attention to your breath slows it down, and that after a while you will feel slightly more in balance. This simple practice of breathing is the foundation of all meditation exercises.

EXERCISE 4: *Paying Attention to the Breath*

Here is a practice that will help you pay attention to your breathing. Notice the rhythm as you inhale and exhale. Focus on keeping the rhythm the same. Give some thought to the physical process that is taking place: The oxygen in your lungs is being transferred to the bloodstream, and when you exhale waste gas is being released. Something like seventy percent of the waste products produced by your body are expelled through the breath.

The next step in this practice can go one of several ways. The two most common are 'breathing light,' which I describe elsewhere, and thinking of a word or phrase in conjunction with the breath. The latter exercise is called by the Sufis Darood. *A Darood is a word or a phrase that you hold in your mind to replace the usual tape-loops of thought that most of us hold in our minds most of the time. A Darood can be any word or phrase, from a name of God such as Allah or Rama or Siva, to a simple phrase like "I am calm" or "I am relaxed."*

Once you've done this exercise, try taking another look at what upset you. Maybe it's not as bad as you thought. Or maybe it is. Either way, something has to be done about it. But what?

Just Say No

I don't want to stray into the territory of the psychologist. If you've discovered something particularly nasty about yourself, you should probably go to a psychologist. To a certain extent, though, spiritual guides can't avoid wandering into the realm of psychology. When we do, our approach tends to be more informal than the psychologist's.

Let's take something simple. You discover that you're too critical of other people. You might be inclined to defend this trait by saying that being overly critical is a manifestation of a desire for perfection. But your job is not to enforce perfection in other people. It is to enforce perfection in yourself. And you are probably just as critical of yourself as you are of other people.

So what do you do? You keep it simple. When you feel an attack of being overly critical coming on, just don't allow it. For a while this may throw a crimp into how you interact with other people. You'll have to find a way around this. I have no idea how you'll do it; that's your problem. Remember, though: keep it simple. You're not performing brain surgery on yourself. All you're doing is noting inappropriate behavior in yourself and stopping that inappropriate behavior. You find it distressing that you behave inappropriately. Other people find it distressing that you behave inappropriately. So don't.

Do not—repeat, DO NOT—tell anyone you're not doing it. As soon as you tell somebody you're not doing it, you lose personal power. There's just one person that you can tell with impunity you're not doing it, and that's your teacher or guide. If they know their business, spiritual instructors will only encourage you in such pursuits.

There is a rule of esoteric wisdom that I've already mentioned. It's even a rule of conventional psychology. You can't recognize a fault or a virtue or anything else in another person unless you possess that fault or virtue or whatever else in yourself. When we find fault with somebody else, what we're really doing is drumming up a melodrama to make our own lives more interesting. The less attuned we are to our inner life, the more likely we are to seek some manifestation of that inner life (or even, however unconsciously, to provoke that manifestation) in the external world.

If you've suddenly seen yourself in what I've said, don't go off on a self-pity jag. Remember that the purpose of this chapter is to more or less casually list several prominent embarrassments we all have, and show how they serve to point out to us what we need to work on in our lives. A little self-criticism is fine. Just don't take it all too seriously.

I'm sure there's not one of you who, in reading what I've just written—that the faults we bemoan in others are the faults we possess in ourselves—hasn't just now had acid-type flashbacks to bits of gossip that you have gleefully passed along. This was gossip that focused on the annoying faults of friends or acquaintances or total strangers. It may even have concerned total strangers or notorious or not-so-notorious public figures. And, probably, you've just now also been brought face-to-face with the unsettling truth that certain of these attributes emanate straight from you. In short, you've had to admit that, like the rest of us, you take a certain vicarious pleasure in witnessing the shortcomings of others, even if these shortcomings are of such a nature that they should only elicit a gentle "Tsk, tsk." The reasons should be obvious to you by now.

Misjudging Your Place on the Path

Another prominent source of embarrassment has to do with how far along the spiritual path we think we are. Either we think we're cooler than we really are in terms of our progress, or we seriously underestimate the degree of coolness we've attained.

It can be hard for us to recognize the first, overestimating, state. We've usually foolishly proclaimed to one and all the high degree of our coolness. Maybe we've suggested that we are certainly the peer of everyone in the group and maybe even hinted that we are advanced enough to teach the group. It takes a lot of courage to back away from a glowing self-estimate of our worth after we have let everybody in on the secret of our greatness.

People who really are spiritually aware tolerate this type of behavior because they know that eventually the exaggerators of spiritual progress will have to face the truth about themselves and some very serious embarrassment will come from this. People who are genuinely spiritually aware understand that this type of misassessment generally stems from a sense of inadequacy. They know that the progress-exaggerators are afraid they don't really know what's going on, or that they are somehow out of the loop.

None of us is ever really out of the loop (or, more accurately, the spiral). It's just that we haven't been able to access the whole loop yet. If you discover that you've been faking your level of self-realization, you'll just have to swallow your pride and go back to being a student. Often, it is then that you discover something wonderful, namely, that those around you are very willing to forgive you totally once you've stopped claiming that you possess something you don't yet possess.

As for underestimating the degree of your progress: this is something I know about only through observation. To tell you the truth, I'm prone to overestimating my own place on the road—which is why I'm able to go on at such length about this kind of misassessment.

When I have students who tend to underestimate their progress, I help them by giving them practices intended to enhance their self-esteem. The following is an example.

EXERCISE 5: *Superimposing a Great Being*

I ask a student to concentrate on a Great Being and see if there is any way in which the student is able to superimpose that Great Being on his or her own being. Another practice that I often employ is to ask the student to walk like a king or a queen, or an emperor or an empress, perhaps using as examples the archetypes in the Tarot deck. (For more information on this practice, see Chapter 13, The Light of Knighthood.*) I may also ask the student to try to experience the being that is presently being unveiled within him or within her. You can try this if you like: What you have to do is* *imagine who you are becoming. This is something athletes do all the time: By methodically visualizing their performance before an event begins, they help themselves to perform successfully.*

If you are of a spiritual turn of mind, you might tend to believe that this process of visualizing your emerging inner self is difficult; we are inclined to believe that such inner archetypes are subtle and elusive and remote from the outward self. Nevertheless, that inner being, however subtly it is manifesting within us, is right there inside us, and we should try to experience it. You won't be totally successful, but that's okay. Just imagine yourself as the whole being you desire to be, and see what happens.

There are numerous levels of commitment and understanding, and just because you suspect yours doesn't measure up to someone else's doesn't mean that it is not significant in itself. The other person may simply be more confident or more verbose or more vocally enthusiastic that you. It's possible she or he is no further along the path than you are yourself.

If you're the vocally enthusiastic sort, reel it in a bit. You're wasting energy. You'd be better off saving it for something more important than persuading yourself and others that your devotion to the path is exemplary. Remember the old adage: Those who know, don't talk; those who talk, don't know. Don't ask about people who write books.

The Higher Standard

We teachers and guides in the lower and middle echelons of the Sufi Order International sometimes do embarrassing things too. I'm sure this is just as true of teachers and guides in other orders. We try hard, however, not to get into one-upsmanship games where people dance the "I can do anything better than you" dance.

Games like this constitute ordinary human behavior, but the things that happen in a spiritual order have particularly deep and dramatic effects, and this kind of nonsense can be more hurtful in our setting than in an ordinary setting. I have been embarrassed and I've embarrassed others. All I can do is forgive the former and beg forgiveness for the latter.

A group like ours is the last place in the world where you should bear a grudge. One of the pleasures and problems of being a member of the Sufi Order International is that we hold ourselves to a higher moral standard than we expect the rest of society to adhere to. The trouble is that we're still a part of that society; it's all too easy for us to forget that we are Sufis and to fall back on old patterns of social behavior.

But it is a source of great delight to us when we do things right, when our behavior makes us worthy of being called representatives of the Sufi order. I can't describe this delight to you—not won't, but can't. It is because Sufis strive to adhere to a higher standard than society as a whole that we can, if we so desire, hail each other in all sincerity as "King of Kings" or "Sovereign of the Universe."

It took me a long time to understand these things.

The closer I get to the upper levels of our order and the inner circle of its leaders, the more I notice that leaders at these levels don't dance the one-upsmanship dance. Each has his or her separate area of responsibility. They all have enough to do without beating up on each other. That doesn't keep the rest of us from trying hard to discover their areas of embarrassment; even Pir Vilayat came in for his share of scrutiny. We can be an irreverent bunch.

Of course, as in any group, what we do is make internal processes manifest. That doesn't always redound to our credit, as the following story illustrates:

A man aloft in a hot air balloon realizes he is lost.

He spots a person on the ground, lowers altitude, and shouts, "Hey! Can you tell me where I am?"

The person below replies, "Yes, you're in a hot air balloon hovering thirty feet above this field."

The balloonist says, "You must work as a spiritual teacher."

"I do," replies the person on the ground. "How did you know?"

"Well," says the balloonist, "what you've just told me is true enough, but it's of no use to me at all."

The person on the ground says, "You must be a spiritual seeker."

"I am," replies the balloonist. "But how did you know?"

"Well," says the person, "you don't know where you are or where you're going, but you expect me to be able to help you. You're in the same position you were in before we met, but now it's my fault."

Schools that teach esoteric wisdom are basically no different from other schools or organizations. The same human dynamics apply; alpha males and alpha females compete with each other while everybody else tries to find a comfortable niche.

There is, however, one major difference between a school like ours and an ordinary school. The nature of our work doesn't allow us to be comfortable. Self-criticism or self-interrogation (Muhasaba) is at the basis of our order, and it creates a dynamic that constantly surprises all of us.

If you feel a twinge of embarrassment, however slight, pushing you in the direction of the spiritual path, follow it. You'll be led to places that once you couldn't have conceived of—places that soon you won't be able to describe.

5

Surrender

All surrender to beauty willingly and to power unwillingly.
                                  - HAZRAT INAYAT KHAN

The word *surrender* doesn't have a warm and cuddly meaning. It evokes images of domination by a superior force, or of our being compelled to do something we'd rather not do. That's in English. Other languages handle the concept a little differently. A Japanese friend tells me that her language has two separate words for surrender. One means what the English word means, while the other signifies the "acceptance of love's enfoldment." Other Asian languages probably make the same distinction. But the connotations in English are the only ones I know, and they always send shivers up my spine.

Maybe the idea of surrender is an easy one for you. As for me, for a long time whenever I heard people in Sufi circles talk about surrender—surrender to the Beloved, for example—my immediate reaction was, "There's no way I'm going to do this thing that I don't even understand!" The phrase "surrender to the Beloved" has a nice poetic ring to it, but to me it always seemed to imply that you were handing power over to whomever this "Beloved" character was.

In fact, that's exactly what it implies. But there are certain words and phrases that mean one thing in common parlance and resonate with a whole other layer of meaning when used in the context of mysticism. "Surrender to the Beloved" is one of those phrases. Surrender to the Beloved certainly has the connotation we customarily assign to it—I mean the ones that send shivers up my spine. But, in the language of Sufism, the meaning is different.

Wahdat Al-Wujud: Sufism's Dual State of Being

In an earlier chapter I alluded to "the place of no thing," a place Pir Vilayat called "the awakening beyond life." My personal experience of this place is limited and I am reluctant to describe anything that I am not completely familiar with. But here goes, and in what follows I rely heavily on what the Sufi metaphysicians have said through the ages. In other words, I won't rely on my own understanding but will try to provide you with the distilled wisdom of others.

In English we try to compensate for the harsh undertones of "surrender" by the phrase "willing surrender." Willing surrender usually refers to a love relationship. Here, though, as my wife points out, we generally mean the surrender of a woman's will to the supposedly more powerful, more magnetic, will of a man. But in this chapter I am talking about surrender in the context of spirituality or religion, and in this context we generally do mean genuinely willing surrender. Even in the spiritual sense, though, surrender seems to imply a surrendering of our puny human will to the all-powerful will of a Creator.

You will have to bear with me now through several paragraphs of metaphysics as I try to lay the groundwork for an explanation of what the word "surrender" means in the universe of Sufism.

You see, for Sufis the word "surrender" has a specific and rather unique meaning. That is because Sufis believe that human beings experience two completely different but mutually interdependent states of being at one and the same time. They call this dual state *Wahdat Al-Wujud*, the Unity of Existence.

Wahdat Al-Wujud is a specific condition, more accurately lack of condition, in which all created things are equidistant from the source and have no existence in and of themselves, but have only the potential for self-expression. Selfness—individuation—is irrelevant to this state. To experience Wahdat Al-Wujud, you have to go beyond the state of reason, beyond viewing reality as discrete bits of information. You have to merge with the void of timeless nothingness in which all things have their source and nothing has separate value.

Follow all that? Good! This is the experience of ultimate unity, one which the mystics regularly fail to describe adequately, just as I'm now failing to do. Pir Vilayat says this state comes before you realize it and is gone before you know it came. Other Sufis describe it as a "place of no thing" or The Blackness. All seem to agree that Wahdat Al-Wujud is "in here" and not "out there." It is in our being, and we attain it not by searching outside but by diving within. It's a difficult state to describe because we are continually forced to fall back on the vocabulary of the normal everyday world to describe it, and Wahdat Al-Wujud is quite beyond our normal everyday world.

Sufis get around this difficulty by resorting to metaphor to describe Wahdat Al-Wujud. The most common metaphor they use is that of the ocean and waves. In our ordinary conscious state, we perceive Wahdat Al-Wujud as waves; we are ignorant that it is an ocean and that that ocean is the source and support of the waves. Though we perceive the waves as discrete objects, they are not separable from the ocean. But, in our preoccupation with the shape, size, color, emotional content of the waves, we completely fail to see the ocean.

If, through meditation and other spiritual practices, we are able to perceive the ocean and merge with it—however briefly and however slightly—the waves recede from our sphere of attention and the ocean begins to become all. This may seem like a desirable state, and it is—except that when we are one with the ocean we can't interact with the waves; we can't get on with the ordinary business of living. Interacting effectively with the waves means giving them the greater part of our attention. This isn't hard when we are unaware of the ocean's existence, because then only the waves are real to us. But when we've noticed the ocean, things are never the same for us again.

Sufis call this state of total immersion in the ocean *Fana* or Annihilation—another word that seems to be negative, but isn't really. I'm sure that in my meditations I've never made it as far as *Fana*, though I understand that there are various levels of Fana, so it's possible I've brushed one of the lower rungs of the ladder of ascension to that state. It's hard to tell about these things. But whatever my own experiences, the description I've given more or less conforms to the descriptions of the Sufi metaphysicians.

What does this have to do with surrender? As you pass through the various levels and planes that lead to the state of Wahdat Al-Wujud, or the Unity of Existence, the word "surrender" takes on a wholly new meaning. It comes to denote the suspension of our disbelief in a reality other than that of cause and effect. Just for a moment, we stop thinking that we can't make the ascent, or even that there is an ascent to be made, and surrender to the infinite space within us that knows the state of divine love for what it is. So you see, surrender turns out to be a love relationship— a love relationship willingly embraced. What surrender is not, is coerced. You surrender because you cannot conceive of any other outcome for your efforts.

Trading Addiction for Love

What follows won't seem to be about surrender. But it is. I'm going to tell you about how I quit smoking. Or, more accurately, how I gave up an addiction.

Pir Vilayat always said that giving up an addiction was one of the most powerful acts we can perform, with smoking one of the toughest to give up. The list of addictions was endless, he said, with his own chief addiction being classical music—not one, he hastened to add, that he was planning to give up.

I believe I was one of the last Sufis in the Western world to give up smoking. When I first joined the order, almost everyone smoked. That percentage was far greater than for the general population; smoking is a tradition among Turkish Sufis and a number of us attempted to carry on that tradition. But our numbers dropped off one by one, until there were few smokers left, only myself and one or two others. I held out until the very end. You might have thought that I regarded myself as the one remaining relic of a bygone era, necessary to the world in the sense that there had to be at least one memento of the Age of Smoking in some museum somewhere.

Gradually I began to see that my addiction was a silly one, albeit a difficult one to give up. Then, suddenly, all the work I'd been doing began to click in. I had found my own personal guide in the order; I'd been initiated as a retreat guide; I had been meditating in a particular way to help myself quit smoking. And my addiction began to ebb. As it did, my libido became reactivated. (My wife liked that.) At the same time my inner commitment to Sufism steadied and strengthened.

What had happened was that in surrendering my addiction to smoking (it could have been any addiction), I became less dependent on the wave aspect of Wahdat Al-Wujud and more open to the inflowing of the ocean aspect. Since that ocean is an ocean of love, love began to manifest within me in place of the waning addiction.

The first thing I noticed was that I began to enjoy friendships more. We like to think that we have plenty of friends and every so often we tally them up. (Come on, I know you do it. Everyone does it, even if only in secret.) We want to be able to declare, if to no one but ourselves, that we have, say, four real friends and a slew of acquaintances—acquaintances who would become friends in an instant if we only expended the effort. Deep down inside, however, we all secretly wonder if any of these people really are our friends in the way that we think we understand friendship. (This leads me to believe that most of us would be happy with just one real friend, if we could figure out exactly what friendship was.)

Our sense of being separate from one another limits the depth of the friendships we can experience. The more we taste of the ocean of Wahdat Al-Wujud, the Unity of Existence—the freer we are of the waves of Wahdat Al-Wujud—the more we are able to see that another human being is not separate from us at all but actually a part of us. That's why, as I freed myself gradually from my addiction to smoking, I noticed a nifty side effect. Friendships were blossoming. These were friendships I'd known were there in potential, but from fear of rejection, I suppose, had never pursued. But as I expanded within I became less worried about rejection and more willing to take chances with relationships.

This has had happy results, and these occurred because I had willingly given myself over to the natural state of surrender.

EXERCISE 6: *Genuflection and Surrender*

How do we cultivate this natural state of surrender? Here's a suggestion: Put your head to the floor at least once a day. You can do this by kneeling or lying down. Make this gesture part of your prayers (as people do in Islam and Buddhism) or make it simply a physical acknowledgment that you are bowing your spirit down before

God. Whatever daily regimen you practice, even if it's only a few minutes of reflection, add genuflection to that regimen. You'll find this very beneficial. Genuflection puts the body on notice that it's not in control; it puts the mind on notice that it's okay to bow down before a higher power; it puts the spirit on notice that you firmly accept certain principles of spirituality; and it literally as well as symbolically puts the head below the heart and emphasizes the truth that the heart is the greater characteristic of our being.

There are other aspects to pursuing the natural state of surrender. I need to preface what I'm about to say by explaining that, for the Sufi mystic, the difference between masculine and feminine has nothing to do with gender. The Sufis regard "masculine" as the creative force and "feminine" as the receptive force. They have given the masculine force the name *Jelal* and the feminine force the name *Jemal*. Between Jelal and Jemal lies the state of *Kemal*.

Kemal may be translated as perfection, but it's a difficult concept to grasp. Think of it as a point of perfect tension. Think of a basketball player who leaps into the air to shoot the ball; there's a point where the basketball player is neither rising nor falling, neither shooting the ball nor not shooting it. This is a point of perfect tension; it is Kemal. When Sufi metaphysicians describe the creative impulse of the divine, they call God the Creator, Jelal, and the Created Universe, Jemal. The meeting place of these two is Kemal, Perfection. As the Sufis see it, you must become feminine to surrender; you must cultivate this Jemal aspect of yourself to be a receptive force.

Moreover, to surrender you must first and foremost acknowledge that you are above all a Being of Light. When you have acquired that awareness, then, when the Beloved reveals to your light a portion of Its light, the natural process of merging gets underway and surrender will come about easily. As Arjuna says in the *Bhagavad-Gita*, "By Thy grace I remember my light, and now it is my delusion. My doubts are no more, my faith is firm; and now I can say, 'Thy will be done.'"

Surrender is no trifling act that anyone can perform. Acknowledging ourselves as Beings of Light is a means of access to this world of surrender. Opening this door, keeping it open, is—or should be—one of the great challenges of our lives. Let me give you a spiritual "light" practice that will help set you on the arduous path to this achievement. This is the first spiritual practice I ever learned. It is simple, it is effective, and it is a practice I still follow. I like simple.

EXERCISE 7: *You Are a Being of Light (I)*

Imagine the universe is a vast ocean of light that is accessible to you. When you've allowed yourself to imagine this, just breathe. Don't pay attention to your breath; just breathe. On the in-breath, imagine you are drawing a portion of the infinite crystalline light of the cosmos into the top of your head. Imagine you are drawing it through your crown chakra down into your heart. (I don't mean your physical heart; I mean your heart center, located behind your sternum.) Once you've drawn this light into your heart, you need to do something with it. So as you exhale, use the intrinsic energy of your heart chakra to transform the crystalline light into a golden light that enhances the light of your aura. There it is: A nice, simple, effective practice anyone can do. Of what benefit is it? Let's look at what you did.

First, you accepted the idea that the universe is basically made of light. You may not be too sure at this point what that means, but you have accepted the idea for now. Then you acknowledged that, just maybe, you could do something with that light. (Or maybe you thought to yourself that you couldn't, and that maybe this is all silliness, but wondered what you had to lose by trying.)

Then you acknowledged that maybe your body was more than simply a mechanism for digesting fiber and protein and carting your neuroses around in. In fact, you acknowledged that it had at least two centers of energy, the crown chakra and the heart chakra. You further acknowledged that these two centers of energy had the potential of doing something important.

Then you acknowledged that you could direct energy with your breath. (Maybe you were just pretending you could direct it, but perhaps you were also thinking, "Hey, what the heck? Maybe it'll work.") And, finally, you admitted to yourself that there is more to you than just your body and that you have an aura whose brightness you can increase simply by using your will.

You have no idea if any of this is true or if anything really happened to you—but it sounds nice and maybe it did work and so maybe you'll do it for at least a little while longer.

EXERCISE 8: *Transforming the Light Energy*

You can increase the effectiveness of the previous practice by adding the following exercise to it. (This next exercise should be done only when you're sitting still.)

As before, breathe the crystalline light of the cosmos through your crown chakra into your heart. At this point, hold your breath and, while rolling your eyeballs up into your head to focus on the third eye, gently place the tip of your tongue on the soft palate. Then imagine that the light you've inhaled into your being has permeated all the molecules of your body, causing them to jiggle and effervesce with the new energy you're supplying them with. Don't hold your breath overlong; there is no need to be uncomfortable. Now, relax your tongue and eyeballs and exhale through your heart, focusing all that transformed light energy through the lens of your heart and flooding your aura with this golden light to enhance and energize it.

It's hard for us to hold in our minds the awareness that we are Beings of Light. This is because we're bombarded every day with the notion that we are a walking, talking, breathing sack of physical matter, plopped down in a universe of similarly constituted sacks, with all of these sacks vying for a piece of the earthly action. Doing practices like the ones I've described will help you overcome this notion.

You'll find it helpful to spend time in the presence of those who are better able than you to hold in themselves the knowledge that they are Beings of Light. It's certainly possible to pursue this goal in a basically isolated manner and, in so doing, successfully improve your spiritual state; look at the many genuinely holy men and women who live the lives of hermits. However, isolation has always seemed to me like a form of self-flagellation. It's not really necessary. On the whole, Sufis limit isolation to a maximum of forty days. (Occasionally, though, an exception is made for those individuals who feel that very long periods of isolation are essential for their pursuit of the spiritual path.)

The Sufi orders have always included very private persons who hold themselves apart (as have other orders). Perhaps spiritual orders are a natural magnet for those who feel themselves to be misfits. I myself have always felt uncomfortable in group situations that focus on intimate matters. I keep expecting to be told I'm doing something wrong. After all, my experience of life has consisted basically of my doing things that didn't jibe with the beliefs of those around me. This naturally created in me a hard shell of resistance that thwarted any attempt by an outside force to change how I acted in the world.

Even those who seem totally at ease in normal social circumstances may be very sensitive and fear the judgments that society renders. I have a number of students who are successful in the world and seem to be at ease around just about everybody, but who, when we're exploring their inner selves together, can no longer hide their affliction: a basic fear of the world.

The Fear of Non-Separateness

Perhaps a fear of the world and its difficulties and judgments is at the core of everyone. This isn't true of those amoral beings for whom other people exist only to be used (or if it's true, it's true in a very different way). I mean it's true for all those basically good people who are trying to figure out who they are and just what they're doing here.

As long as we behave as separate discrete entities with clearly delineated boundaries—entities who busily defend our personal space including our psyches—easing those boundaries will be quite a challenge.

That is why, when we try to think of ourselves as Beings of Light, we feel a sense of danger. Our boundaries seem to become diffuse; there is no longer enough skin to separate us from other people; there are only not clearly defined rays of light that all too easily mingle with our own rays. Often, as we sit in meditation with others working on light practices like the ones I've described above, we suddenly realize that everybody around us is doing exactly the same thing; we realize that everybody is commingling with everybody else, that we are no longer separated by absolute boundaries. Then we become very daunted, very uncertain, because all along we've been counting on these boundaries to guard our personal secrets and maintain our sense of uniqueness.

However, if we can allow ourselves to accept the wisdom of the Sufis (and other spiritual groups) and sink into the vast sea of individuals who are intermingled even while they know themselves to be separate individuals, then we will encounter one of the greatest treasures of life: the company of kindred spirits. You'll discover that you've surrendered to an immense reality where your brothers and sisters support you. This realization contains the seeds of great power; were we all to access that power, we could take giant strides toward healing the fundamental rift between us that the illusion of separateness creates in every society.

As you pursue the spiritual path, you'll notice that you have fleeting experiences of what I've described above—experiences that your ingrained defenses make you instantly try to reject. One powerful defense we've erected around ourselves is the one that protects us against being hustled. Our lives have taught us that new experiences should be regarded with suspicion. When we sense our light-beingness commingling with the light-beingness of others, we become apprehensive. "This feels too good to be good for me!" we exclaim. Or, "Somehow—I haven't figured out how—I'm being hustled and something bad is about to happen to me!"

This is a natural reaction. It's your psychic defenses automatically kicking up a fuss at an experience you don't understand. After all, you've worked hard at becoming a discrete entity, and all of a sudden your inner being is asking you to lay aside that hard-won armor and become (or recognize that you already are) a crystalline structure of light. That's a lot to ask. Be gentle with yourself as you go through this. If you have a spiritual guide, continually check in with your guide to have your progress monitored.

The Yearning Switch

We are back to the subject of that willing surrender which comes when the yearning for the Beloved has become so overwhelming that nothing else can quench the fire of the love we feel. Our need to merge with the ocean of union overrides all other needs and desires, and becomes the only thing possible for the loving beings we are.

You will have come across the sentiment I've just expressed if you've read the poetry of the Sufi saint Rumi. In fact, that feeling pervades all of the ecstatic literature that Sufis have created over the centuries.

If you want to share in that yearning, you have to ask yourself: "How do I turn on the Yearning Switch?"

It's a good question. It's one I asked myself for years. And then, one day, my Yearning Switch turned on, all by itself—perhaps not as intensely as the paragraph above would suggest, but it was definitely on. Today, my inner pull toward union has become an imperative I cannot deny, nor do I want to deny it. But how I managed to turn on the Switch, I have no idea.

The longing for the Beloved is in every one of us. In one sense, it is the desire to return to the cosmic womb, to the source of all our being. That yearning runs closer to the surface for those who are mystically inclined than it does for the rest of us.

But even the mystic must undergo a certain amount of training—and of un-training—to be able to access and eventually surrender to this yearning.

One of the themes of this book is that we can and should allow that yearning to manifest within us and take its place as part of our experience of existence. The Yearning Switch has lain unactivated within us all along. The difficulty lies not in constructing it—it's been there all the while—but in finding out where it is so that we can turn it on. How do we find it? You might try putting your head to the floor and asking God where it's located. Make this a daily exercise. Eventually an answer will begin to unfold.

Ultimately surrender is the renewal of the vow of service we took before we became incarnate. We are spiritual beings, paying a visit to this planet to experience, to manifest, to evolve. Before we came, we took a vow that once born we would fulfill our original, pre-birth purpose. It will help us to do so if we can see this world as a place of learning, if we can surrender to our soul's desire to know itself and its Creator.

Now, put your head to the floor!

6

Getting on the Path

He is brave who courageously experiences all things; he is a
coward who is afraid to take a step in a new direction; he is
foolish who swims with the tides of fancy and pleasure; he is wise
who experiences all things, yet keeps on the path that leads him
to his destination.   - HAZRAT INAYAT KHAN

I was chatting with a friend the other day when he suddenly asked me: "What happens when you're pursuing
the spiritual path and you actually get to a certain level
of enlightenment?"

"Beats me," I said. "It probably means more work."

"I'm serious," he retorted. "What happens when you
become a mystic?"

I looked at him. "You used to say you were one," I
said.

"Not anymore."

Then I understood. "You're saying your horizons have
just expanded," I exclaimed.

"I guess that's it."

We went on to talk about how this abrupt expansion of his inner horizons was affecting his view of the world. At any given point in our lives we tend to think that what we know is what there is, subject to minor technical modifications, and my friend had just had this point of view radically adjusted. In other words, whatever our view of the universe may be, we tend to think of the boundaries of what we can perceive of it as set in stone or at least carved in wood. We may pay lip service to the idea of expanding our consciousness; we may admit that there are people around us whose consciousness is much more expanded than ours is—though not by much! We may even acknowledge that there are extraordinary beings in the Himalayas and other remote areas who are in touch with God-consciousness, the Universal Mind, or whatever. But when we're actually pressed to try to broaden these frontiers within ourselves, we likely cry out, "I can't do that, and even if I could, I'm not sure I'd believe that was what was really going on!" And we leave it at that.

Our mind doesn't want to believe that frontier-broadening is really what's going on. The idea is too upsetting. This was the case with my friend whose horizons had just expanded. He'd had this wonderful experience of a change in spiritual location, and it had left him confused. He'd discovered that there was more to everything than he'd thought; his consciousness of the world had been ratcheted up a notch or two, but he didn't know how to deal with the "moreness" of things he was now experiencing.

His family wasn't happy with him either. He had changed and, despite his best efforts not to change, he was acting differently—and even spiritually sophisticated families have a hard time accepting aberrant behavior among their own and get confused when they encounter it.

We do our meditations; we read spiritual books and grapple with the ideas in them; we attend lectures and seminars given by people we admire and respect—we do all these things and still, when the time for transformation comes, we are caught by surprise. It's one of the more fascinating aspects of this whole spiritual process. Part of it, I believe, stems from our love of, or need for, ritual. Whatever our present station (a station, or *Maqaam*, is the level of our spiritual realization or awareness), we tend to erect ritual around it. That ritual can affect the way we dress or the way we walk or the body language we use— probably a combination of all these things. And once a ritual is established, even if it's only two weeks old, we assume it has permanence.

Another factor is that once we have gone through one of these transformations we may not be at all eager to repeat the experience. It is, after all, pretty exhausting. That transformation and that new ritual formation that follows it do take a toll.

Memory and Persistence

What attitude should we take when we encounter stumbling blocks along the way? (In particular, the ones I've just cited.)

Pir Vilayat always had the same answer to this question. He told us that we must always push through, push through our doubt, push through our fear, even push through our elation. I liked the directness of that approach—though personally I also like sneaky, as in not letting your psyche know what you're planning to do. My guide, whom I will just call A, says something I like. That is simply, "Remember." This answer is so simple that it took me a long time to figure out what she really meant. I finally realized that she was saying, in effect, "Remember who you are when you are stretched to the limits of your capabilities—the limits of which even you cannot know."

I believe memory is the key. At difficult junctures, we need to summon memories of past spiritual accomplishments: of fine meditations performed as flawlessly as can be; of personal retreats where we attained something unexpected; of the current of love that can pass between friends while in meditation. All of these memories, and many others besides, create a core of remembrance that can sweep us up and carry us through the trauma of a change of station, a change of *Maqaam*, and support us as we create new rituals that sustain us until we arrive at the next level.

In spiritual circles we speak of being "on the path." That phrase is a convenient misnomer. Our entire experience of life from birth to death is one of being on the path. Life itself is a journey, and everyone, whatever his or her spiritual status, is on that path; whether we've awakened to the knowledge of that journey is irrelevant.

What we in spiritual circles call "the path" might more properly be called "the response" or "the reflex." Something, let's say it's the soul's desire to know itself, wells up from deep inside us and we respond. Since in most cases the call comes in a voice or style that is unfamiliar, we tend to respond inappropriately. One of the most common inappropriate responses is the belief that what has just happened to us is more important than it really is. That isn't to say it's not important. It is, because it is happening to us, and we are the most important person in our universe.

But try to keep things in perspective. Here's a basic rule: If you can reproduce the experience anytime you want, that's a good thing. But if it happens once and you can't reproduce it—well, that's fine, but don't take that particular experience too seriously.

Pir Vilayat had a wonderful line that always brought us all back to earth. It was, "You're chosen not because you're the best, but because you're the best available." In other words, some master or angel—whoever manages these affairs—has looked at the available talent and decided that the best she or he can come up with is you. I personally find this idea heartening. I'm not expected to be Mahatma Gandhi, just me.

You may also experience feelings of awe, terror, elation, ecstasy, remorse, and the absolute conviction that you've gone insane. All of these reactions, and others like them, are responses to an inner process that is really very natural.

We in the West have little feeling for the naturalness of these phenomena that stem from the spirit. We want to label what's happening. We want to compartmentalize it. We want to fit it into the Western scheme of things. We think of such experiences in two ways: (1), They're evil, and want to eat us alive; or (2), They're holy, and will save our souls. Aliens in science fiction stories usually fall into one or another of these two categories, thus reflecting society's tendency to think that something out of the ordinary is either an invasion of merciless aliens or the coming of a new Jesus Christ.

Rarely does it occur to us to see something unusual and unknown simply as something that hasn't yet been defined. If we can stay with the feeling that something strange that has happened to us is simply something we don't know about, we are ready for the next step: doing something about this new experience.

When the Call Comes

What do you do when the insistent call comes? Run to your priest or rabbi? That might work, but unless these individuals are schooled in mysticism and know what to do when, say, you feel the opening of your *kundalini*—that core of psychic energy that is coiled up at the base of your spine waiting to be released—then they are not going to be a lot of help. I will grant you that the number of clergy who are trained in mysticism is increasing, and maybe you are lucky enough to have access to one. If so, he or she will certainly be able to tell you what to do.

How about seeking out a therapist? That is the commonly accepted thing to do when a person is experiencing something outside the norm. It might work—if the therapist understands spirituality.

Talk it out with your mom or dad or best friend? Maybe you'll get lucky; but more often than not you'll be worse off than you were before, because, as a rule—not always—your family and friends won't want you to be anybody other than the person they rely on to reflect their own natures and values. And if that's sad, it's also true.

Find a teacher? There are a zillion of them out there, just waiting to sell you crystals, meditation tapes, bio-feed-back machines, et cetera. Very few of them have a clue about what constitutes spiritual practice. Some may be sincere, but they may not have much on the ball. They can be sufficiently bright, however, to take you for all your money—and what does it say about you if you let them do this?

I'm not being totally fair. You can look upon all these people vying for your spirituality dollars as part of the spiritual development of our planet. If you want to spend your money that way, go ahead. But once you've gone beyond what I call the Unicorn Phase of spirituality—dealing with eccentric people and practices—you'll need a legitimate teacher. Legitimate teachers know what they are doing, and are concerned, not with a growing balance in their bank accounts or an increase of their personal power, but with your spiritual progress.

You won't get far on the path without a genuine teacher. All of the prophets and masters were blessed with such a teacher. (Just check the history books.) I tried to do without a teacher for years. The idea of putting myself under somebody else's thumb really bothered me. I read books on spirituality. I pretended to meditate. I told everyone how cool I was. But it wasn't until I met Pir Vilayat and asked him to be my teacher that things began to fall into place for me. I won't belabor the point, except to say that every esoteric tradition accepts the basic premise that a teacher is essential for spiritual progress.

How do you find such a teacher, once the call from within has come?

Be patient. Recognize that you don't know yourself as well as you thought you did. Otherwise, you'd have known that that inner voice existed. Patience is a supreme virtue here. Know that the teacher will come. The classic formulation for this is: For every step the student takes toward the teacher, the teacher takes ten steps toward the student.

But patience has a downside. You've begun to glow from within—and the beacon of your internal flame is beginning to draw to you every spiritual wacko within 1,000 miles. Your real teacher will not arrive at your door immediately and say, "Let's go!" First of all, you will have to work your way through this wave of wackos. It's as if your future teacher were hanging out there in some spiritual dimension waiting for you to learn discrimination.

You still have to seek out your teacher yourself, even if your teacher is drawing you to him or her. It's a joint responsibility. Be patient. Have your purpose clearly in your mind. Be calm. Then the person you seek will come.

Let's say you've found a real teacher. You think you resonate with this person, and you say, "I want to be your student. Please initiate me."

The teacher says, "No."

You have two options. You can stomp off in a huff, convinced that the teacher made a mistake and that one day you'll show this teacher where to get off.

Or you can insist.

If you stomp off in a huff, the teacher was right to refuse you.

If you insist, and the teacher finally says okay, the teacher was checking you out.

But if, despite all your insisting, the teacher still says no, you need to find out why. Generally, there are two possible reasons. The first is that you approached a teacher of the wrong spiritual persuasion as far as your own growth was concerned. You needed, say, a Buddhist, and you encountered, say, a teacher of Vedanta.

The second possibility is that what you really need is a therapist.

Generally, though not always, the teacher will tell you why you've been refused. Be prepared to do some research into the differences between the various disciplines.

Teachers can be quite uncanny when it comes to figuring out who should be their students. I knew a woman who repeatedly asked one of Pir Vilayat's sheikhs to initiate her. He kept refusing. Finally he told her he would initiate her on one condition, that she cleaned up her apartment. I don't know how he knew her apartment was a mess, but cleaning it up was the condition he imposed.

Weeks went by, then months, and she didn't clean up her apartment. A group of female Sufis finally went by to help her. But even as she thanked them profusely for coming, she blocked their every effort to help her clean up her apartment. To the best of my knowledge, she still hasn't been initiated. What she really needed was a therapist. To the best of my knowledge, she still hasn't seen a therapist. I hope she has cleaned up her apartment.

Have I upset you by mentioning therapy? Just because you've received the call doesn't mean you're stable. Certainly I wasn't. The recruiting angel apparently doesn't care about emotional stability. Nevertheless, esoteric work absolutely does require emotional stability. It's a mystery to me why the recruiting angel isn't hip to this, but that's the way it is. If the teacher says, "Go get some therapy, then come back and see me"—do it. If the teacher says, "I really think your path is with this Ute shaman who lives in Santa Fe," go see that Ute shaman. In the final analysis, it's okay. We all belong to the same family.

Once you've been accepted by a teacher, say thank you and do what the teacher says. Don't ask the teacher to reorganize your life. Don't ask the teacher to fix your finances. Don't ask the teacher to talk to your boyfriend or girlfriend whenever you two have an argument.

What is your teacher's job? It is to give spiritual advice.

In Sufism, there are two distinct schools of thought regarding the relationship between the teacher and the student. One school of thought holds that the teacher should know everything there is to know about the student, while the other maintains that there should be a certain detachment between teacher and student. The debate has been going on for millennia. It will probably never be resolved, especially as the approach that is adopted is very much a function of the teacher's personality. My wife and I know quite a lot about the lives of our students, but when it comes to issues of a personal nature, we strive for absolute neutrality. We try to follow Pir Vilayat's dictum of never giving personal advice. This works for us.

When you embark on the Sufi path, you are usually given basic instruction and one or two personal practices. Then the real work begins, that of keeping your mind on the training and actually doing the meditations you've been assigned. At first this may seem relatively easy. And in a way, it is. Normally you're simply asked to do practices that take up no more than fifteen or twenty minutes of your day. Usually you're asked to do these in the morning. Often these beginners' practices consist of the repetition of a single Hindi or Sanskrit or Arabic word or a set of words. This may seem odd at first, but you'll get used to it, and it isn't really all that difficult.

Here's the problem: the practices actually work. Your personality begins to change. This can be annoying because the change is so subtle that you scarcely notice it—until the day comes when you find a good excuse for skipping meditation, and then find a good excuse for skipping the next mediation, and then the next.

This is the first hint you have that your personality is rebelling; the practices have been acting on you very subtly, and your personality has been reacting just as subtly to try to remove these annoying new influences from your life.

Love, Service, and the Need for Transmission

In Sufism, we distinguish between the path of love and the path of service. It took me a long time to understand the difference between these two paths of spirituality. In the beginning I couldn't understand why some people melted at the sight of Pir Vilayat. They would sit in rapt attention through his talks and at the end they wouldn't be able to remember a single word he said. To be truthful, I still haven't quite figured that out. At the time I pored over explanations in books, saying to myself, "Oh, so that's why! They are on the path of love, and devotion to the teacher is the focus. Later this can change to devotion to God!" But I still didn't really understand.

Now, however, I can see that there are people who are drawn to a particular spiritual order because of the leader's charisma. These are the people who pursue the path of love. At the same time, there are a smaller number of people who are drawn to a particular order because they have realized that this is where they will be able to carry on the work of serving people, serving the community, serving God, that they know is their purpose in life. Both paths are equally valid; the first is the path of love and the second is the path of service.

There's no particular merit in being on one path as opposed to the other. The right path is the one you're suited for. Your path suits you and it feels right, and that's all the reason you need. If being on the path begins to feel wrong, you should get off and go back to what you were doing before. Many do, and this is fine. Remember, though, that the discomfort you experience may stem from your ego's protests about the journey. If that is the case, this is something you have to work on. I've known people who have never had a moment's doubt about the rightness of the path they're on—but I haven't known many people like this, and sometimes I've had my doubts about how they really felt. The student who questions and doubts all the time is far more common; doubting and questioning are as much a part of the spiritual path as paying attention to your meditation.

A final word about why there is so much insistence on having a teacher and joining a group. That word is *transmission*. There is a certain amount of information and experience that the student can receive only by sitting in front of someone who has already received that information and experience and who then transmits it to the student. This may sound like hocus-pocus, but it actually works.

Furthermore, you need a teacher because you do not really know where you are going or how you are going to get there. As Hazrat Inayat Khan expressed it, using a mundane simile from navigation:

> One may attain the purpose of life without a personal guide, but to try to do so is to be like a ship traversing the ocean without a compass. To take initiation, then, means entrusting oneself in regard to spiritual matters to a spiritual guide.

In other words: you might make it across the ocean without a compass, but you probably wouldn't. So why try?

A third reason why you need a teacher—and you'll have to trust me on this one—is that in a spiritual order the student and the teacher establish a kind of magical connection that exists nowhere else except in this kind of relationship. The student-teacher relationship is a completely unique way for two human beings to be together, and once you have experienced it you will be very reluctant to let it go. Additionally, you connect with the line of transmission that flows through the ages. This may be even more important than the individual connection.

But finally you are the one who is responsible for yourself. If you choose to go off on your own, then so be it. If you decide that your path really lies in working on your career and you want to save that spiritual stuff for later, that is what works for you. Your decisions are what shape your life; they ARE your life, and they are your responsibility alone. But to receive the call to spirituality is a great blessing. In my opinion, it is a great shame not to respond to such a call.

If you do respond, the blessing will go on and on, in ways that you cannot foresee but which you will never regret.

7

Back to the Future

The whole Cosmos moves as a pendulum: the past and the future, transciency and eternity, human and Divine. It is out of the ever-constant back-and-forth dialogue between these two poles that the future is created. I believe that the future is not just something waiting for us; it is something that is built by sorting through the past for that which belongs to tomorrow; it is a continual work-in-progress that takes place in every era and that occurs through each individual's innovative, imaginative, and conscious participation. It is what I call spiritual evolution.
- VILAYAT INAYAT KHAN

When Majida and I got married, the sheikh who performed the ceremony said: "The most remarkable thing about your relationship is that you two actually found each other."

I took this to mean that maybe there's no foolproof predestination scheme operating in the universe—that maybe there's a degree of randomness. When I combine the idea that none of us has one set future, with the Sufi concept that all past, present, and future events exist "now" in the ocean of being of Wahdat Al-Wujud, I have to conclude that we all have "memories," not just of one, but of many possible futures. These are potential memories; some have more potential than others, but all are nonetheless merely the future in potential. I believe that it is the presence of these potential "future memories" that gives rise to the experience in our lives that we normally call *déjà vu*.

Hazrat Inayat Khan once said that the dream world has the same reality as this one. It's only because we are so involved in this world and think we are cut off from the other, he said, that we don't believe the other world has the same validity. Pir-o-Murshid went on to say that the worlds that Sufis call the Djinn world and the Angelic world have the same validity as this world. We are cut off from them essentially because we are asleep to these worlds. It's only the mystic, he added, who, with inspired vision and growing skills, awakens to them.

What Hazrat Inayat Khan said about the equal validity of all realities suggests that while *déjà vu* is an interesting peculiarity of existence on our waking plane of time-space reality, it's a constant and common staple of the awareness of the true mystic. Probably in that sense it is very helpful, although it occurs to me that a never-ending hail of *déjà vu*'s in your life could be rather annoying.

Once, when Majida and I were in India managing a tour group for Pir Vilayat, we were fortunate enough to be invited to a session with Baba Sitaram Das Onkarnath. Baba has since passed, but was at that time one of the greatest living saints of India. Baba spoke only Gujarati, but he had an able translator. After instructing us for about a half-hour, the great man had to stop. He protested that the astral plane was so noisy that he was having great difficulty concentrating on this plane of existence. Pir Vilayat later told me that he almost could not look at Baba because Baba's aura was so bright. I guess there's a downside to everything.

The Arrow of Time

Pir Vilayat had an exercise that he offered to help the student find his way through the psychic minefield represented by all those other planes of existence that, having the same reality as ours, are constantly impinging upon us but of which we are not—usually—consciously aware. He called this exercise the Arrow of Time, and explained that it operated on the principle that the pull of the future is stronger than the push of the past—that the being that you are becoming draws you to find the path to its fulfillment. Pir Vilayat writes:

> The Sufis have developed a metaphysics of time and fate dramatically different from the ordinary, linear perception of time. For instance, they distinguish between the moment when the past overlaps the future in a way that inevitably shapes it, and a simultaneously occurring instant when the forward-moving arrow of time is intersected by a transcendent dimension—like an infusion of fresh, uncreated energy into circumstances that have become fixed and stagnant.

Let's focus for a moment on only one part of this statement. It takes courage to believe that the being you are becoming draws you to find the path to its fulfillment. Why courage? Because the being you are becoming is so much greater than the puny self you imagine yourself to be. Looking at your future self, at this far more complete and integrated self you are becoming, can be an embarrassing and intimidating experience. It is the rare individual who can look at this self that is coming, understand what is happening—and look upon all this as a promising experience!

This person you're looking at, your future self, is essentially a stranger. Spiritual teachers are constantly perplexed by the problem of how to convince students that it's okay to move out of who they are into who they are becoming. That's why there are so many stories about teachers who put students through ordeals leading them to a "psychic shock" that propels the student into change with impunity.

The teacher has to be both astute at recognizing when the student is ready for the shock and creative in the application of that shock. I used to say to myself—after Pir Vilayat had nailed me several times with psychic shocks that were essential to my progress—"What can he do to me now that I won't see coming?" My psyche had become wary and watchful. But, fortunately for me, Pir Vilayat never lost the ability to surprise me even when I had already sensed that something was on the way.

The Dangers of Precognition

I do not think that we can force the future to reveal its intent as far as the self we are becoming is concerned. Perhaps some of you out there know how to do this, but I am not aware of any exercises that can lead to this objective. All we can do is ride out the waves of information that come rolling in from the future. Please remember, if you can, that a precognitive capability—an ability to know the future beforehand—is a side effect, not a desired result. In fact, the ability to know the future can cause a lot of trouble, because almost no one will believe what you've seen, including yourself. But such skepticism is probably a good thing since, as I've already suggested, all futures are potential. We do not know which particular bits of precognition belong to our time-space world and which are a part of the vaster reaches of the multi-universes.

I know someone who has doom and disaster visions frequently. Usually, she will find herself in a place or a building and know—be absolutely certain!—that something very unpleasant is about to happen in that place or building. Generally, she ignores these visions of doom, thinking them to be a manifestation of her incipient claustrophobia. (She gets nervous in confined spaces.)

But when she has a vision of something bad and then it happens, she remembers that she had the vision. She has told me that two days before the 1993 World Trade Center bombing she dreamt she was there, in the World Trade Center. She felt terribly uncomfortable, and felt as if she urgently had to get out.

More frequently, my friend is aware of something unpleasant that is about to happen to someone. Sometimes, she's aware of the impending death of that person. Obviously this is the kind of information that, when it comes surging through you, will not give you peace of mind. What my friend finds particularly confusing is that most of the things she sees don't happen. She's had to learn to distinguish between the subtly different gradations of power of the various visions that she receives. She can pretty much tell now when an event has the possibility of actually manifesting. But it's taken her years to sort all this out.

As is so often the case with aspects of spirituality, precognition is a very subtle phenomenon, hardly an "in-your-face" kind of a thing. That's why we do not even notice a great deal of the information we get. If we do notice something, we tend either to ignore it or to give it much more weight than it probably deserves. I'm not talking about those genuine psychics who are very tuned in to aspects of creation outside of time and space. They are an entirely different breed, and have a whole other set of problems they must deal with. I'm talking about those persons who, from time to time, look around and realize that they've been in this situation before, or they think they have. This probably happens to everyone, but when you begin to recognize your spiritual sensitivity, you become more aware of this sort of information coming in. Why? Because you are looking—sometimes desperately—for proof of that strange reality that seems to be overtaking you.

When you look for that kind of knowledge, you will find it.

8

Authenticity and Watchfulness

It is the soul's light which is natural intelligence.
                                        - HAZRAT INAYAT KHAN

When I was a young man, serving in the Army in Korea, I decided to join a skydiving club. I really had no idea what I was getting into, but the idea seemed glamorous and daring. I went through ground school, where I learned the theory, how to pack a parachute, how to fall, and the myriad other things you need to know to be safe and enjoy yourself.

Then, after the required classes, I was permitted to go to the drop zone for my first jump. It was easy. All of the sensations were so new and exciting that I did not have the sense to be scared; I was just completely thrilled. I made a second jump that day; then I was scared, but I did it anyway, overcoming my fear and continuing to make jumps. I made one hundred and twenty jumps in all over a three-year period. That isn't many jumps by skydiving standards, but was a lot for me, as jumps are expensive and I have never been one to have a surplus of disposable income. After a while, I stopped.

Little did I know back then that some fifteen years later I would be listening to Pir Vilayat tell people they should do something dangerous in their lives, like skydiving or rock climbing. They should do this, Pir Vilayat said, because it's important for us all to test our courage. It was then that it occurred to me that skydiving and meditation are pretty similar in that in both you take a step into the unknown and put your life—or, worse still, in the case of meditation, your ego—on the line. In fact, skydiving and meditation share three steps: 1. you suffer some anticipatory worry, usually very heavy; 2. you plunge into the unknown; and 3. after having plunged, you assess what has happened.

In some ways the leap into the unknown is easier for skydivers than it is for meditators. When you skydive, at least the jump is right there in front of you; you can see what you're doing and all you have to do is decide whether to jump or not. On the other hand, in spiritual matters you usually have no idea when to jump. Usually you don't even know you've reached the place on the spiritual path where a leap of faith is required.

It's no exaggeration to say that we encounter bouts of worried anticipation along that path. I'll tell you about a couple of my own worries that continue to pop up. First, there is the absolute conviction that my spiritual guide is seeing right through me and in the next moment will find out that I am completely worthless. A second is the sense that something awful is about to happen to me. On the other hand, the feeling that nothing AT ALL is going to happen to me—and never will—is almost as bad.

We often feel uncertain about how far along the spiritual path we are capable of going—that is, how high a skydive we have it in us to make. In order to deal with this fear (and the fear of being seen through or experiencing something awful or nothing at all), we need to keep in the forefront of our mind the thought that all the practices and all the meditations we do serve just two purposes:

- To slowly and steadily reprogram our personality;
- To prepare us for the moment of transformation.

When you're reprogramming the personality, you have to take into account the anticipatory nature of the ego. In meditation (as in skydiving), the ego protects itself against what's coming by creating a scenario—any scenario. But since the ego is just as clueless as the personality, it really has no idea what's coming. You constantly have to keep in mind that the great mass of expectation it is producing is usually highly misleading.

We guides often hear the disgruntled question: "Why isn't anything happening? I've been doing this practice for three years and nothing has happened yet." Even as the person is saying this, we guides are gazing into his or her face and observing that it is positively glowing with spiritual energy, even though that person obviously has no clue about the transformation that has been taking place within.

It's as if we're protected from being arrogant while on the spiritual path by a lack of awareness as to the point we've really reached. Let me illustrate with a story.

Pir Vilayat met a *sannyasi*, or Hindu holy man, traveling in the Himalayas. The sannyasi told the Pir that when he put on the saffron-colored robe of a mendiant spiritual seeker, he was obliged to search out a place in which to meditate. One of the vows you took in this tradition was that once you'd chosen a place of meditation, you stayed there whatever happened. This sannyasi wanted to begin his practices far from civilization. He searched for a long time until he found what seemed to be the perfect place: a beautiful valley with a fine cave, water within walking distance, and an abundance of fruits and vegetables. There were no signs of predators. The sannyasi formally vowed to remain in this place until he found the Self.

Just then, the unmistakable cough of a tiger echoed through the forest. The holy man was immediately certain that he had made the wrong decision.

The sannyasi hid in the cave for two days. On the third day he waited until midday, hoping the tiger would be holed up somewhere to avoid the heat. Then, no longer able to control his thirst, he rushed down to the stream, filled his container, and turned back to the cave.

The tiger stepped out on the path in front of him.

The sannyasi's first impulse was to flee. But he knew that would be pointless. His next thought was to race for a nearby tree and climb up it to escape the tiger's claws, since tigers can't climb trees. Once the tiger was gone, he would be able to flee from the valley.

But what about the vow he'd taken not to leave the valley until he found enlightenment? If he broke this vow, how could he ever expiate his sin? He truly did not know what to do. He was terrified of the tiger and wanted to flee, but he was equally appalled at the idea of breaking his vow.

All at once a calm descended on him. He decided that he had taken a vow and that, whatever the outcome, he would be faithful to that vow until the end. If God had decided he would best serve humanity by being eaten by a tiger, then so be it. Having made his decision and overcome his terror, he stood his ground and watched calmly as the tiger approached.

The tiger padded up to him. Slowly it rubbed its long powerful body up and down the sannyasi's thigh. Then it escorted him back to the cave.

Thereafter, until he attained enlightenment, the sannyasi shared the valley with the tiger.

Getting Away from Backing Off

You can see that the personality of the sannyasi had no idea what was going on, while his spirit knew enough to wait quietly and simply accept whatever happened. Taking a vow is a serious thing. The mystical tradition is full of stories about what happens to initiates when they make a vow—when, as we say, they "take hands." But it's here that the experience of the skydiver begins to separate itself from the experience of the initiate. The skydiver usually floats quietly to the ground. The initiate usually gets to watch his or her life fall apart, and have the pleasure of participating in that collapse.

If your intention has been serious, this collapse is merely appearance. What is actually happening is that Who You Really Are is emerging. It is confronting Who You Think

You Are, which has an abundance of unenlightened notions. This is a messy business. Generally we are very attached to Who We Think We Are, and will defend to the death that version of ourselves.

To maintain your balance during this difficult time, you need to be in a constant state of watchfulness. Let us suppose that after a great deal of hard work and introspection you actually find yourself poised at the edge of this dangerous, if metaphorical, abyss. You gaze into its depths and say, "No way!" You back off, abandoning all the hard work you've done to make it to the edge of the abyss.

You'll back off many times. I've backed off myself. It took me 15 years just to realize that this was what I was doing, and another ten to figure out what to do about it.

What to do about it turned out to be very hard and very simple at the same time. We see ourselves, primarily, as others see us. We spend a great deal of our time conducting ourselves in a way that validates the view that others have of us—or that we think they have of us. When we begin to take responsibility for our actions, one of the most important things to pay attention to is Who We Really Are as opposed to who other people think we are. That distinction is fairly simple to grasp. The harder part is continually paying attention and catching all of the moments when we forget that we are personally responsible for our own being.

After you work your way through all this, however long it takes, and fight your way back to the new point of departure—then you jump. Or maybe you don't jump. Even at this point, you can still back off and think about it for a while. Eventually, though, if you are to be true to your vow, you take this plunge into the unknown. Once you have taken the plunge, you may turn around and look at where you jumped from only to discover that it was a little mound, not a high cliff. You leapt two feet, not into an abyss. That is not to say, though, that the leap hasn't altered your life profoundly. Hazrat Inayat Khan says,

> It is only those who are blessed by perceiving the origin and source of all things who awaken to the fact that the real inclination of every life is to attain to something which cannot be touched or comprehended or understood. The hidden blessing of this knowledge is the first step to perfection. Once awake to this fact, man sees there is something in life that will make him really happy and give him his heart's desire. He can say, "Though there are many things in life which I need for the moment and for which I shall certainly work, yet there is only that one thing, around which life centers, that will satisfy me: the spiritual attainment, the religious attainment, or, as one may even call it, the attainment of God."
>
> Such a one has found the key to all happiness, and has found that all the things he needs will be reached because he has the key to all. "Seek, and ye shall find; knock, and it shall be opened unto you. Seek first the kingdom of God, and all these things shall be added unto you." This kingdom of God is the silent life: the life inseparable, eternal, self-sufficient and all-powerful. This is the life of the wise, whatever be the name given to it; this is the life which the wise contemplate. It is the face of this life that they long to see; it is the ocean of this life that they long to swim in. As it is written, "In Him we live and have our being."

Honoring the True Self

The deeper we delve into spirituality, the more we are forced to examine what we do. The more we do that, the more aware we become. No one else need know about those objects of embarrassment we increasingly come across. But we know. Sufis call this embarrassing and necessary examination of our conduct Muhasaba.

In carrying out this constant examination, you honor the true self. Your inner self does not need reasons to exist. It wants spiritual freedom, and it's up to Who You Really Are to provide it. To honor the true self is simple. All you need to do is admit that you yourself—you, the personality—do not know what the self needs. Something inside you, though, does know. That "something" is what ultimately controls your life. The experience of this inner self is one of glory, and its being is innocence, and it exists in each and every one of us.

Pir Vilayat says Sufis are the ambassadors of God. Certainly, then, we must accurately assess what constitutes our true self and our true position in the hierarchy. It is difficult to be objective in making this assessment. That is why we need a guide. Here's a story to illustrate my point.

A thousand years or so ago, a sultan was extremely fond of a certain Sufi sheikh. So enamored was he of this sheikh that he asked the sheikh if he could become his student.

"No," replied the sheikh. "You are not ready."

The sultan was very upset by this rejection. He lobbied the sheikh's other students, asking them to try to persuade the sheikh to accept him as a student. This they did, and the sultan finally relented a little. He told the sultan he could come live in the *tekkeh* (Sufi community house, another word for a khanaqa). The sheikh added, however, that he would not initiate the sultan. Furthermore, the sultan would have to agree to do whatever the sheikh asked.

The sultan accepted these conditions. He thought that by living near the sheikh he would be able to demonstrate his own wonderful qualities and thus hasten the day of his initiation. He was very pleased with this arrangement, until he found out what duties the sheikh had in store for him. He would be the kitchen scull, the lowest of the low, cleaning the greasiest of the pots, taking the garbage out, performing the most repugnant forms of manual labor.

The sultan had never done anything like this before. But he was determined. He decided to persevere and do the best he could. All went well for a month as he resolutely went about his duties—which duties were very far removed from anything he had ever done as the ruler of his country. The other students watched his conscientious conduct and began to sympathize with his plight. They went and pleaded with the sheikh on his behalf.

"He does whatever you ask," they pointed out. "He should be considered for initiation."

"He is not ready," said the sheikh. When the students protested, the sheikh added, "Let me show you that he is not ready."

The sheikh arranged a demonstration. When the sultan took the kitchen garbage to the dumping place, the sheikh and his students watched the sultan from a place where he could not see them. As soon as the sultan left the tekkeh, a young boy, following the sheikh's instructions, darted out into the street and collided with him, knocking him down and scattering the garbage everywhere.

The sultan jumped up and screamed every sort of invective at the boy. Then he gathered up his garbage and, grumbling all the while, continued on his way.

The sheikh looked at his watching students with an "I told you so" expression on his face, and then returned to his work.

Another month went by. Again the other students pleaded the sultan's cause. Again the sheikh replied that the sultan was not ready. Again, he had the boy collide with the sultan as he was carrying out the garbage, and again the sultan responded with anger.

This time, however, he did not scream at the boy. He merely muttered under his breath as he picked up the garbage and went on his way.

A third month passed. The students, impressed by the sultan, approached the sheikh once more. Sighing, the sheikh said, "Let us see." He set the test up once again. The boy ran out, the sultan fell, the garbage spilled, all as before. The only difference was that this time the sultan simply picked up the garbage silently. His face showed no expression. His demeanor said only, "I have this task to complete."

The sheikh turned with a smile to his students.

"Now he is ready," he said.

As far as I know, this is a true story. The sheikh was Sheikh Abul Fazl Fusail bin Ayaz and the sultan was Sultan Ibrahim Adham Al-Balkhi. Bin Ayaz is the fourth sheikh of the lineage of our order. Al-Balkhi is the fifth. We recite their names in our silsila—a list of the sheikhs and pirs who have led our order since the time of Hazrat Khwaja Ali, the nephew of the Prophet Mohammad.

For years I watched people get upset because they thought they were ready for something and Pir Vilayat thought they were not. For a long time I thought getting upset like this was a peculiarly American phenomenon. But after hearing the story I've just told you, and reading many accounts of the lives of the ancient Sufis, I've come to the realization that this kind of spiritual standoff has been around in many different places for a very long while. I've realized that, as painful as we may find it, we really do need to accept the assessment of the individual to whom we entrust our spiritual life.

This is not to say that we accept blindly—not at all. It's much better to pay attention to what we are told and to examine our reactions to this. Sufism is a path of self-discovery. The teacher merely instigates the discovery.

EXERCISE 9: *Avoiding Gossip*

Here's an exercise. It seems easy, but it will try you to the very limits of your soul. (My students know this and groan whenever I assign it.) It is simply this: Avoid all gossip for one week.

If you think this is too easy, take it a step further. For one week, don't talk about anybody who isn't in the same room with you.

You have my guarantee that you will realize great benefits from this exercise!

The Opening of the Heart

When I first became part of the Sufi Order International, I was puzzled for a very long time by the statement that Sufism is the path of the heart. It made no sense to me. I was equally puzzled by the statement that we must continually strive to open our heart.

Open your heart? That sounded good to me, but how did you do it? I didn't want to look like a dummy, so I never asked anybody exactly how to do it. I just kept on doing the practices I was given. My thinking was that, if my heart ever did open—whatever that was—I would probably know it. I suppose I thought this opening of the heart would be accompanied by fireworks and maybe dancing girls—chaste ones, of course—and much rejoicing in heaven and lots of other nifty happenings that would let everyone know that I now had an open heart.

Well, I waited, and I waited—and nothing happened. I kept on doing my practices and going on personal retreats and absorbing other experiences as they came my way, but this open heart stuff continued to elude me.

After a while, I just stopped thinking about it and concentrated on other things.

What I had not taken into account was the subtlety of what those of us in the Sufi Order International really do. I had thought I understood it, but I didn't, not really. Usually at the end of a retreat Pir Vilayat would say something to us like, "We have talked a lot about the inexplicable," or, "Words are totally inadequate to describe this," or words to that effect. I can well remember the first time I heard him express this thought, and the smug "Well, of course" I felt at the time. But I didn't really understand. But, as the years went by, I began to understand that he was saying no more than the simple truth. Words indicate, point, perhaps give clues, but they cannot actually *describe* experience. So the phrase "opening of the heart," that I was trying to understand with my mind, kept eluding me.

And then it happened.

I was taking a personal retreat when my heart opened. Actually, it had been happening all along; I just hadn't noticed it. My retreat guide had given me a very difficult practice and I was having a lot of trouble getting it, and so day after day she kept giving it to me. I was determined to master it if only to move on to something else—when all of a sudden I had this very clear image of a sun in my heart, shining a brilliant golden orange and radiating out from my chest and back. At the same time, there was a second image: that of the "white hole" that the Pir speaks about as being in the center of our being.

Did I care about any of this? No; all I cared about was learning how to do this annoying practice. So I sat there in the retreat room shining like the sun and ignoring it because it was not nearly as important as what I was doing. After the retreat was over, I still hadn't mastered the practice to my satisfaction. But I noticed that the glowing heart still seemed to be hanging around. I was both relieved and disappointed to find that nobody else could see it. It occurred to me that I might finally have gotten one of those open hearts, but it wasn't nearly as spectacular an event as I had expected, so I wasn't quite sure.

The glow lasted for about a month and then gradually faded, so that the day came when I wasn't aware of it anymore. While it was still there, though, I would look down at it from time to time and wonder what I was supposed to be doing about it. I never did come up with an answer.

Such was my experience, and you're probably wondering why I've even bothered to tell you about it. My point is that my inability to recognize what had happened to me was probably just another guy thing: I had already acquired an open heart, but I couldn't admit it to myself, because this very valid experience of mine was clothed in such a—to me—hokey description. I have always been able to feel people intensely and to know their truth. That is no big deal. It's what I do. But I could not accept this particular terminology. So I guess God gave me this experience—or maybe I somehow invented it for myself—to show me how silly it was to reject an experience out-of-hand just because it was clothed in a description that did not sound manly to my ears. Over the years, I've seen many people get hung up on definitions and phraseology while ignoring the truth behind the definition and the implications of that truth.

The Unimportance of Experience

A word about telling other people about your experiences: You may tell your guide about your experiences, but no one else. The reason for this is that you want to avoid comparing your own experiences with those of others and finding fault with your own as well as theirs.

Let me put it as simply as possible: Experiences don't mean much. There is a story about a student named Shamcher Bourse who was initiated into the Order by Hazrat Inayat Khan and served as his translator and secretary for a time. Shamcher had risen to the title of murshid. He was once asked about the kinds of spiritual experiences he had. He replied that he had faithfully done his meditations and practiced *dhikr* (the remembrance of God) for forty years, and that during that whole period he hadn't had a single "experience." "But," he concluded, "dhikr made me what I am today."

In our order dhikr is more often spelled *zikr*. In the *Message Volumes* of Hazrat Inayat Khan, there are more than thirty references to zikr and only two to dhikr. They are the same word. Dhikr is Arabic, zikr is Persian. Since we are an order originating in India, where the Sufis came in with the Persian-speaking Moghuls, we tend to use Persian words. Pir Zia, the present leader of the Sufi Order International, uses the word zikr.

Zikr is the basic practice of Sufism. The word literally means "a remembering," and encapsulates the central purpose of Sufism, which is the remembering of ourselves and our place in the universe. The practice consists of the repetition of a sacred word or phrase. The words repeated most often are *La Ilaha Illah 'llah Hu,* which mean "nothing exists except God, Hu."

We tend to think of spiritual experiences as a sort of payoff for hard work, or at the very least a little bit of recognition for our efforts. If it appears that somebody else is getting a better payoff than us, then—well, you know where that can lead: in absolutely the wrong direction.

Non-Intentionality: Expecting Nothing

This brings me to the important subject of intention. I have already said that there is no compulsion in Sufism. But I've also said that there IS compulsion in Sufism, in that you have no choice. At some point, a student of Sufism has to come to terms with this paradox. You practice Sufism because you have to—but you don't have to. I once asked one of our sheikhs if he ever thought of quitting the order. "Sure," he replied. "But where would I go?" And that pretty much sums it up. As annoying and as frustrating as it can be to pursue this path, you cannot imagine yourself doing anything else. And, if it is true that you are both compelled and not compelled, you truly have no choice but to do the best work you can.

To do the best work you can, you have to pay attention to your motives. You'll recall that earlier in this chapter I defined the practice of Muhasaba as a constant self-questioning, a constant "What am I doing?" So, ask. Look at how you are doing your meditations and see if you can decipher your motives. Are you simply going through the motions and fulfilling some sort of duty? Are you expecting a payoff? Both of these are pretty normal motives for proceeding; they have been mine, and they will be yours.

For example, there is a practice called *Quddus*. Quddus means Holy Spirit, and the implication is that you are trying to align yourself with the spirit of God. When you've been doing the Quddus practice, it's hard to avoid thoughts like, "So when do I get to see the Holy Spirit? I mean, come on, I've been calling out your name for six months now and you still haven't put in an appearance. Is that really fair?" But your motive shouldn't be to call forth the Holy Spirit. You shouldn't be expecting anything at all.

You want your intention to be as pure as possible. Keeping intentions pure requires work, just like anything else. As soon as an expectation or an opinion is layered onto a practice, that practice loses its effectiveness. Chanting for personal wealth is probably not a Sufi reason for chanting. Let me further refine the notion of intention. It can best be described as controlled surrender. You have a feeling, perhaps vague, that you aspire to something greater than yourself. What that something might be is unclear. Nevertheless, the power of this feeling compels you to do something. You must hold onto that feeling as the prime motivator—you must not allow it to sidetrack you into an emotional dead-end—and if you do manage to hold onto it in that way, you will find that you are slowly able to surrender to it further. The important thing is not to get too excited about the effect this might have on you. There are dozens of stories about students who did their practices for fifty years and never felt a thing, but who in the process became beloved of all the people in their village. You may not feel anything, but other people surely will. Just be careful not to ask them what effect you're having. Remember what Al-Hujwiri said about praise?

As you can see, intention can be a fairly complicated business, because you are continually having to examine yourself for selfishness. Actually, most Sufis have no problem with selfishness, believe it or not. It requires a certain selfishness to do what we do; it requires a certain paying of attention to the self to the exclusion of all else. Sufis do, however, have a problem with—let me see. What did Pir Vilayat call it? Oh, yes. Concupiscence. You can look that one up. Think of it as your homework, figuring out where your concupiscence is and what you can do about it.

9

Creativity: Walk Like a King

When the artist loses himself in his art, then the art comes to life.
- HAZRAT INAYAT KHAN

As a woodworker, I love few things better than lathe work—"turning" a beautiful chunk of wood into a beautiful bowl or other round object.

But lathe work is the most difficult and frustrating of all the woodworking skills. I've been turning for ten years now, and I've only just begun to feel I can truly create something beautiful when I practice my skill.

I still approach a valuable piece of wood with hesitation. It's not that I'm worried about the price of the material, which can easily run you $100 a pound for a piece of rare walnut burl. It's that I hesitate to violate the potential of a unique and beautiful piece of virgin wood. For example, I have a large piece of maple burl that a friend gave me. Maple burl retails at $5 a pound; my piece weighs at least fifty pounds. I turned one bowl and it came out nicely but the rest of the piece sits on my shop floor beside the lathe, waiting for my next burst of courage. Even though this piece of burl was free, I don't want to mess it up.

When I decide to toss a piece of wood on the lathe and have at it, something wonderful happens. The anxious "I" goes away and I just create. Once you've made the decision to apply tool to material, the path is set. I'm never totally sure what will come out of these woodworking sessions. All I know is that I've placed a piece of wood on the lathe and the end-product will be bowl-like. Beyond that, anything can happen. Usually I'm innocent of intent.

I believe true creativity requires this innocence of intent. You create for creation alone, and not for anything you might get out of it beyond the process of creating, such as praise or money. I'm not dismissing praise or money, but for our current purposes they are beside the point.

Neither am I saying that you don't need skill. When I fasten a piece of wood on the lathe, the skills I have assiduously acquired through the years kick in. Simply wanting to create a beautiful object isn't enough.

I'm not saying you shouldn't pay close attention every instant. Did I mention that the lathe is the one woodworking tool that can kill? There are others that can eat your fingers off and even take away your arms, but if a twenty-pound chunk of wood comes flying off the lathe spinning at 1,000 r.p.m., you'd better not be standing in the way.

But true creativity is something that comes from deep within. It is at one and the same time a conscious and an unconscious process.

Such is also the case with the practices and meditations that come when you travel the spiritual path.

The Three Kinds of Spiritual Creativity

There are three kinds of creativity in spirituality. The first is that of the artist. Since the woodworker is—or should be—an artist, it's the kind of creativity that enables me to transform a beautiful piece of wood into a beautifully rounded object.

The second kind of creativity, closely allied to the first, is the kind of creativity that enables you to remold your personality. This is the basic hard work of spirituality that you find out has to be done once the process of awakening has begun within you.

Thirdly, there is the kind of creativity that is the act of joining with the universe in the process of creation. This can be thought of as Self-realization, or doing what you do when you have finally arrived.

In all three, there is a powerful element of having to learn hard skills, but at the same time you have to forget all about that and simply be.

We encourage beginners on the spiritual path not to be too creative. We do this not because we think beginners lack ability or potential, but because beginners lack the requisite expertise and technical information. In spirituality, there are no twenty-pound chunks of wood that come flying out at you and kill you. But doing something foolish in spirituality can mess you up for a time or send you down an inappropriate path. So it's best for you to pay attention to your guide and learn the rules, before you try to break any of them. (Someone like Pir Vilayat is at the other end of the spectrum; he discovers the rules, such as they are, and when he comes back from a retreat and announces that he has discovered some new combinations, everyone grabs a notebook and listens hard. The rest of us lie somewhere in between these two extremes.)

Following the spiritual path does involve a lot of time. Maybe that's why ecstatic poetry like that written by the great Sufi poet Rumi is so popular: somehow the confrontation with our smaller self doesn't seem so tedious when Rumi describes it so beautifully. But in spirituality as in everything worthwhile, patience is the key—patience, and the basic assurance of your own worth and of your capacity to effect meaningful change within yourself.

EXERCISE 10: *Walk Like a King*

Imagine yourself as the sovereign being who you really are. (This exercise is akin to Exercise 2, "Imagining the Master.")

When you walk, walk like a king or a queen. When sovereigns walk, how do they view the world around them? I am talking about that royalty that takes full responsibility for all that it governs and that knows it is the servant of all that it surveys, while at the same time knowing that it is due a certain deference.

In the U. S. today, we have created an entire society based on the idea of littleness. What if we were to regard one another as royalty? If I defer to your sovereign soul, and you defer to mine, this creative act will completely change how we think and feel about each another.

First, though, you must glimpse the fundamental reality that you are a sovereign soul, royalty, a king or a queen. Then you will know how you should see others, and how others should see you.

So, walk like a king.
Walk like a queen.
Walk like a sovereign soul.

Know your sovereign soul for what it is. That is the great creative act with which you will begin your journey along the spiritual path.

The next part of your spiritual training is the long hard work of reprogramming your personality. You began with the act of visualizing your greatness. I am going to give you some exercises that will reinforce that vision. But first I need to tell you a bit more about what I mean by reprogramming the personality.

Reprogramming

Pir Vilayat adamantly insisted that we never totally lose our personality or get away from our individual quirks. What we do as we move along the spiritual path, he said, is soften those quirks; we begin to see them in all their unreality, as no more than dream impressions. At the same time, we begin to honor them.

Our objective is not ego eradication. We want to re-align the ego so that it assumes its proper place within the totality of things. We certainly do not aim to have the ego control all of our actions. Our goal is to admit that there are areas of inappropriate behavior within us. These areas need attention. There are surprises in store for us when we find these areas, many of which we can't get to unless we change. Our objective is to come to the place where we can admit that what we really desire is union with the

Beloved and that we are prepared to do whatever is necessary to achieve that union.

When we're faced with all these warnings, admonitions and hard work, our natural response is to deny that there is anything that needs to be changed. It's one thing to listen to the inner call; it's quite another to mess with something we have gone to such lengths to create—namely, our personality. And even while we politely agree that, yes, we see the necessity of restructuring our personality, on an unconscious level we fight that decision tooth and nail.

EXERCISE 11: Fana-fi: *Dissolution in the Being of Another*

Here is another exercise that can help you and that can be done any time. This practice is similar to Exercise 2, "Imagining the Master," and to Exercise 10, "Walk Like a King." It is known as fana-fi. *Fana-fi refers to the dissolution of the self in the being of another. For this exercise, imagine that you are sitting facing another human being. Ideally, this person is your spiritual guide. If you haven't got a spiritual guide, imagine a spiritual being whom you greatly admire.*

Once you have imagined facing this person, imagine that you are facing a series of progressively greater spiritual beings. The stages of greatness have names; you ascend the spiritual ladder. In fana-fi Sheikh, *you dissolve in the being of the Teacher. Next comes* fana-fi Pir, *in which you dissolve in the being of "an Elder," the head of an order. A further step upward is dissolving in the archetype of the Prophet,* fana-fi Rasul. *At last you are at the stage of dissolution in God:* fana-fi Allah.

You work through the same process at every stage. It's not an easy process. Imagine you are sitting in front of the guide you have chosen, visualizing that person in his or her highest state and totally accepting the being of that person. Once you've become comfortable with this process, superimpose the features of the guide on your own features. Take the mantle of the guide's being and allow it to flow over and within your own being, as if you were becoming the being you are imagining.

Next, assume the personality of the guide. Feel that you can react as that person reacts, feel as he or she feels. Finally, enter into the consciousness of the guide. Make it your own. If you cannot, at least gain a deeper understanding of the reality of that consciousness. Make sure that you firmly grasp the reality of one stage before you move on to the next. Once you have "become" one being, continue.

There is another way of doing this practice. You can concentrate on an object rather than a person. Essentially it's the same practice, without the difficulty of the human personality. Choose an object you find beautiful. It can be a flower or an elegant piece of pottery or anything of that sort, but its basic form must be simple; it should not be a complex arrangement of lines and colors, as in a painting.

Let's take a rose, for example. First, look at the rose. Then close your eyes and see the rose in your mind's eye. Open your eyes and look at the rose again; then close your eyes and see the rose in your mind's eye once again. Continue to do this until the image in your mind's eye is solid enough that there is no drift or fading. Hopefully, you will be able to do this naturally, without straining.

The next stage consists of imagining what it's like to be the rose. The stage after that consists in imagining "roseness." In the stage after that—the final stage—imagine the essence of flowerness as it exists throughout the universe.

When I give this practice, I generally tell the students to do each stage for at least a month. If they have trouble moving up the ladder, I tell them to go back and start over again.

Responsibility

Responsibility is another aspect of spirituality that falls into the category of creativity. I've tried to avoid bringing up the subject of responsibility, since no one ever likes to talk about it. I'm afraid, though, that the time has come to broach the topic.

So far I've talked about how you can know where you are on the path and how you can defend yourself against your own silliness. Both of these are commonly encountered pitfalls as you travel the spiritual path, and there are many more of a similar stripe.

A student of spirituality must have a sense of responsibility to the spiritual hierarchy and to all humankind. This sense of responsibility is a force, but a secondary force. The driving force, the primary force, is love.

When I bring up the subject of responsibility in class, my students cringe. It's as if they're saying, "Can't we just stick with the easy stuff, like a nice simple seven-level meditation, and not do responsibility?" They react this way because taking responsibility implies doing something, and in this hectic day and age people don't want to add more things to their "to-do" lists. I'm not saying people are irresponsible; I'm saying that they find it difficult to think about responsibility.

I was talking with a student the other day about her great desire to go to India. She had decided not to go because she felt her spiritual work was here in the U.S. She felt that traveling to India would be like eating spiritual chocolates—tasty, but not nutritious. She felt, in fact, that her trip would be rather selfish.

I understood. For her, traveling to India would have been going back to the past. A tradition of mysticism has to be built up here in the West, and those of us who are on the construction crews take our work very seriously. We need to create an entirely new mysticism, one that melds East and West into a whole new synthesis. To do this, we must look to the future; that is our responsibility. Those of us who are "middle-management" spiritual teachers are beginning to get a hint of the colossal task ahead. It may take seven hundred years to do what needs to be done; such is the resistance of materialism which has its own built-in incentives and rewards.

Usually when I tell people about the seven hundred years they reply, "Okay, then. Guess I'll go back to worrying about myself and just ignore that long-term nonsense." Unless you have a mind that thinks in terms of time-frames that are practically geological epochs, my mission statement probably won't make sense to you. There's no reason why it should. Still, those of us who think in terms of geological epochs would like you to try to understand.

EXERCISE 12: *You Are the Mystic*

Let's return to one of the practices I've already described, the one in which you imagine yourself as you would be if you were deep into the work of the mystic.

See if you can actually think of yourself, in your mind's eye, as being that mystic, the one you mentally see sitting in front of you. It will seem to you that such a person has certain powers of manipulation that you presently do not have. What would you do with these powers if you had them? Where would your responsibilities lie?

Let's take another tack: What would the mystic be thinking? What is he or she contemplating? How does the mystic look at her or his fellow beings? Pir Vilayat gives us a clue when he writes, "When we judge others, we are certainly judging the Artist who has created them. If we realized this, it would not be difficult to feel the presence of God everywhere."

Meditate on this phrase. See how it applies to your personality and your life. Make a point of trying to refrain from judgment. In this way, you will slowly begin to create the being you imagine you can be.

You have begun to co-create with God.

When people are initiated into the Sufi Order International, they are told never to assign themselves a practice. Why? Because we are the worst judges of our own state. Looking at yourself, you won't see the forest for the trees. For the longest time you won't even see the tree for the branch. You will need an outside observer. Don't be offended; this is true of everybody. It was not unusual for the Pir to ask people he trusted to be honest with him about what he himself was doing or how he was teaching. And, of course, he had his own spiritual guide. If the Pir could submit to this discipline, so can you.

God-Realization

I'd like to conclude this chapter with a few words about attaining God-Realization. Needless to say, I approach this subject with extreme caution. I'm hesitant to presume to say very much about it at all. I don't want to create the impression that God-Realization is something that can even be talked about. It is not, not any more than the color blue is something you can discuss with someone who has been blind from birth.

Nevertheless, despite my disclaimers, I will say this: God-Realization is God's realizing you, not your realizing God. Few people go to the extreme of allowing God to realize them. Why? I suppose because finally it is extremely difficult, almost impossible, for us to break our attachment to separation.

People who don't attain God-Realization are no less valid than those who do. They simply don't participate in that area of creative reality. Those who will one day attain God-Realization are driven by a sort of inborn compulsion; that's all. As I've said, what you do is what you yourself need to do. As long as you do whatever you need to do, that's fine. The important thing is your presence and your openness to God.

What is the role of your spiritual guide in helping you achieve God-Realization? The guide expresses the Beloved's experience of physical reality—or, as the Sufis call physical reality, *Nasut*. The guide tries to look upon you with the love of all Creation. You will sometimes see that look of love in your guide's eyes and may feel that it is enough just to bask in that warmth. On the other hand, you may be one of the very few who needs to see what the guide sees. If you are, your need will be a a mighty force pushing you to the edge of what it is possible for humans to experience. Then you become what Pir Vilayat called the Co-Creator. Once you are a Co-Creator, God looks directly through your eyes and acts purposefully on the earth plane. There is no pretending about this state. It is the real thing.

So, as I so often advise, watch your breath, do your meditations, and wait and see what comes.

Your fate is in your own hands.

10

The Retreat

The spiritual knowledge is never taught. Even the initiator
cannot teach it in words; it is imparted, and that comes without
words.   - HAZRAT INAYAT KHAN

It was late 1998. I was headed down the highway in
my fifteen-year-old Plymouth Voyager van on my way
to an individual two-week spiritual retreat where I would
entrust my soul to a guide I did not know very well.

And I got lost.

I never get lost. I always know where north is, and east
and south and west. They had me teach map orientation
in the Army because of this skill. But now, on my way to
this retreat, driving fifty miles an hour instead of my usual
sixty plus, asking myself twice as often as usual, "Am I
doing the right thing?"—I got lost.

I stopped the van, looked at the map, figured out where
I was, and continued on my way.

Was getting lost a kind of symbol of the unknown territory I would be getting into with this unusually long, and solo, retreat? Probably not, I thought. Probably it was a sign of the anxiety I was feeling. Still, even though I'd had a lot of retreat experience at this point, I knew this retreat would be somehow different. Knowingly approaching the unknown can have that effect.

At 3:30 that afternoon I pulled up in front of the modest ranch house where I was to spend the next two weeks. No one was home. My guide had told me she wouldn't be back until four. Actually, I had deliberately arrived early in order to reconnoiter the place by myself. The feel of a place you go to on a retreat is important; it has to be a psychic space that is appropriate to your soul. I decided the feel of this place was fine. The front yard was neat, but not fussily so. The neighborhood was unusually quiet. I walked around to the back of the house where the retreat hut was supposed to be. There it was, a building 8 by 10 feet. It was painted white and tucked into a corner of the yard. I opened the door and went into this one-room cubicle I was to occupy for two weeks. It had a cot neatly made up with an unpretentious quilt, an electric heater, a small table that obviously served as a kind of altar, and an electric tea kettle. That was it. The walls had recently been painted white but there were no decorations. I would come to appreciate this lack of decoration; no decoration equals no visual distraction. I approved of my new quarters and went back to the van to get my bags.

Once I'd carried my things into the hut, I took out my camera. I'm an amateur photographer. I like taking photos, and I wanted to give my personality something to do.

The personality acts up at the beginning of a retreat; it doesn't want to be doing this in the first place; it feels challenged, even threatened. The personality hates change and I had come on this retreat to see about some changes. At times like this you have to trick the personality into cooperating. You have to soothe it and distract it, and so I was letting it take pictures.

I stopped taking photos when my guide arrived. I will not describe her. For purposes of this retreat, she did not have a personality; she was my guide. She invited me into the main house for tea and conversation, but it soon became obvious, even to me, that my ability to converse was fading away rapidly in the light of the forthcoming experience. It wasn't long before she showed me where things were, explained the routine to me, and deftly deposited me back at the retreat hut.

I approved of her style as much as I approved of the hut, and I knew that this was going to be a good retreat.

It had to be. I was hoping to transform myself. Not that I had expectations. You have to try to have no expectations when you go on a retreat; otherwise, your expectations will interfere with what can happen. But transforming myself was my subliminal intent.

I had made extraordinary preparations for this retreat. I had quit smoking two months before, in part so that I wouldn't have the baggage of cigarettes to drag into the retreat. I had started rising at 3:00 a.m. to meditate—that's a practice recommended in spritual circles, anyway. I had brought nothing to read and I had decided I would write nothing. I would not listen to music even though I knew that, as a popular adjunct to meditation, music would be offered. I was going to stick to the normal retreat diet, though I knew that if I insisted I could get more varied fare; there would be no coffee, no animal products (no meat, no dairy, no eggs) and no spices.

There would be no talking at all. All communication, at least on my part, would be by written note only; the no-writing vow would not be broken if the notes were restricted to essential communications like, "I'm out of granola" and so on. The no-talking vow included avoiding contact with anyone but my guide, as much as that was possible. Even contact with my guide would be restricted to our having a short daily meditation together, usually in the evening just before dinner. In the days to come, I would learn to appreciate the way my guide and her husband respected my vows. Whenever I entered their house—to use the bathroom was the usual reason; sometimes I would be replenishing my eating supplies—they would disappear behind closed doors. They were sensitive to my whereabouts and always made sure to avoid me in my rare comings and goings, and I really valued that.

An important part of the retreat process is how much personal baggage you leave behind. I'd never left so much behind before. This was the first time I'd given up cigarettes. At previous retreats, I'd always taken a book to read—a respected Sufi text, of course! (I think of myself as a reader. That's part of my idea of who I am.) At previous retreats, I had always taken copious notes. I'd usually finagled a way to have coffee in the morning. But all this had meant that, although I was doing the prescribed practices, I wasn't really doing the retreat.

This time, I was really doing the retreat.

So there I was, fully prepared, with vow in hand and support system set aside, ready to begin. And that's what I did: I began. Nothing dramatic, nothing difficult. I was given a list of practices and I started doing them.

As regimens go, it wasn't bad. It went like this:

- Rise at 6:00 a.m.
- Go outside and wait for sunrise. While waiting for sunrise, do pre-sunrise meditations.
- Do fairly simple meditation and purification practices until 8:00 a.m.
- Have breakfast. Take a shower. Get back to work.
- Do meditation and other practices until noon.
- Take a two-hour break. Take a nap and maybe a walk.
- Do more practices until 6:00 p.m. Be ready for the guide to come and give the regimen for the following day.
- Have dinner.
- See a movie. No, I'm kidding about the movie! But I had had a hot meal.
- Meditate until 10:00 p.m.

Does this sound easy? Bear in mind that, except for my brief and infrequent contacts with my guide, I was alone in a one-room hut (or just outside it, sitting in an armchair) for twenty-four hours a day. Furthermore, I'd made an agreement not just to be alone but not to seek anyone out, not even an all-night grocery store clerk. I had a great many odd things to do, like repeating words for an hour at a time in a foreign language, usually Arabic or Sanskrit, occasionally Ancient Greek or Hebrew. Sound easy?

Try it. I'll let you off easy and give you some English words. Try repeating this for an hour: "Toward the one, united with all." Go ahead, try it. I'll wait.

The personality hates all this. I did discover (as I'd earlier discovered, on shorter retreats) that if I allowed the personality to kvetch while I more or less ignored it, then it was happy and I could get on with my work. After a few days on a retreat, the personality gets bored with itself and stops—or slows down, anyway. It still pops up from time to time with a remembered slight or some other complaint, but mostly it stays quiet. In my case, eventually—after eight or nine days—it actually began to enjoy the discipline. For the experienced meditator, as for the neophyte, all of this is a struggle. Everything worthwhile is. You just mustn't let it bother you.

Eventually, the retreat ended.

I had the obligatory post-retreat assessment session with my guide. Then I got into my antiquated van and drove back home—at my usual speed of sixty miles an hour, not fifty. I wasn't half as worried as I had been when I was coming. And I didn't get lost.

Then I was back in my old life—but with a difference. I had just done something that very few of my acquaintances will ever understand or even know about. Witness this conversation.

"Hey, Phillip, how was your vacation?"

"Wonderful! I went on a retreat."

"Really! Uh...what's that?"

If you do a retreat, your re-entry is likely to be similar. You'll get to the point that I am at now, where you just tell people where you went; you don't tell them what you did there. I have to say, though, that I'm getting much freer now about revealing what I do. So are other Sufi friends of mine. We have the impression that, even in the Western world, some people have finally reached the point where they like to know that some Westerners are seriously pursuing an inner life. Even then, most aren't planning to emulate such a pursuit. They admire someone who goes on a retreat, though, in the same way as they admire the priest or rabbi who prays for their souls.

Perhaps you're thinking that I've left something out. Are you wondering what happened to me during my retreat? Are you wondering if I was transformed?

It's not quite true to say that when I went on this retreat I was looking to be entirely transformed. I wasn't looking for anything. As I've already mentioned, when you go on a retreat you should have no expectations at all. Expectations get in the way. The most effective way to do a retreat is to decide at the beginning to do the work and just let whatever comes, come. The retreat can have a goal, or a theme, like healing or entering into a sacred space. Even if it does, though, you're merely providing a focus, not positing a result. The instant you prejudge result, you've lost that result.

Moreover, you are not in charge of matters as much as you might think. The Quran says: "God raises up who He will." That's why, for the purists, doing the retreat is its own reward. I am not sure that I subscribe to this view myself, but it may be helpful to keep it in mind.

So, no, I definitely did not go into this retreat expecting to come out of it a clone of Saint Francis of Assisi. (Well, the thought may have crossed my mind. I'm only human, and I can't be completely sure. But I knew that the chances of my being transformed in this way were very slim.) Nevertheless, something did happen to me—though I am not particularly anxious to tell you about it. I have two reasons for this.

1. I have never experienced anything that is any different from what thousands of other mystics have experienced, and they have written about it far more eloquently than I ever will.

2. The only way for you to understand what I am talking about is to experience it yourself.

But perhaps I will lift the veil a little for you.

Imagine yourself sitting in a small one-room retreat hut following a disciplined routine such as I have described above, and arriving at a place where your personality finally gives up protesting and agrees to go along with you in this bizarrely aberrational experience you are having.

What do you feel?

You feel very calm.

It might have taken you eight or nine days to get to this state—not eight or nine days of increasing wonder and awe as the blessed state comes ever closer, but eight or nine days of, "Why in the world did I ever agree to do this (occasionally punctuated by the exclamation, "Oh, that's why!")?"

I can only speak for myself, and perhaps your experience will be different. But there can come a point in the retreat when total relaxation seems to be the most natural state in the world. This is relaxation at a level most people never experience, because they are never able to escape from their worldly cares long enough to do so. Body, mind, emotion and soul are in harmony; all of them are comfortable and glowing. At moments like this you begin to suspect that there may be something behind notions like the "One Being." "Maybe this is all true," you say to yourself. "Maybe I really am a part of a greater whole, a greater whole that I, in turn, encompass."

So I'd like to list some points to keep in mind that may help you attain success in any retreat you take. But before I do, bear in mind that my retreat of fifteen days, all alone, was an unusually long and stringent one. The student of Sufism usually begins the retreat experience with a three-day retreat. I often have a first-timer do just two days. After a few two- or three-day retreats, the student advances to a six-day retreat. Six days is considered the time period for an annual maintenance retreat. Most people stop at six days, often for purely practical reasons. In modern society, it is difficult to find the time to devote more than a week solely to yourself. Every time I go on a retreat, there is a part of me that feels a little guilty at abandoning Majida for a week—not that she's ever given me any reason for thinking I should feel guilty.

Anyway, here are the points that you might want to remember.

• Attitude is all-important. Your attitude determines what sort of a retreat you have. If you want your retreat to be transformative, your attitude has to be one of total submission. I'm not saying you should be a wimp, or involved in a masochistic relationship with God. You don't even have to give up your opinions, though a strong suspicion that they may not be valid would be helpful. I am saying that, in this context, total submission means allowing the power of the practices and meditations to work on you while at the same time you firmly separate yourself from your day-to-day support systems.

• Along with maintaining the right attitude, you must allow yourself to retain the capacity for being surprised. There's a kind of innocent honesty—a sort of naiveté, I suppose—that carries us forward when opinion and knowledge hold us back. When Majida and I do our retreats, we try to simply do the assigned practices without thinking much about anything else. Thinking about the other things is the job of the retreat guide.

• At the end of this process, there may be God-Realization.

Again, remember that God-Realization is not something you strive to attain, or even something you seek. God-Realization is not about your realizing God; it is about God's realizing you. To put it another way: you try to get good enough at the meditations that you acquire the capability to step aside and allow a direct experience of God's realization of God's own Self to occur through you. Since this requires that you no longer be present as a discrete volitional entity, most people are uncomfortable even with the idea, let alone the reality. And admittedly it does require a certain calm assurance on your part that you will get your mind and body back! It can take a great deal of work to arrive at this place.

On the other hand, sometimes it just happens. The great Sufi metaphysician Ibn 'Arabi is said to have attained God-Realization within three days of his first retreat, when he was eighteen years old. "Well, goody for him!" you might feel obliged to say. Remember that we each have our own path and we each have our own personal expression of the divine. Comparisons only cause distress or, occasionally, arrogance. So learn to relax, discover repose, and let's see what happens.

• Here and there throughout this book, I talk about Muhasaba, the continual examination of conscience. The constant practice of Muhasaba will help you to know, at every point, who you think you are. Such knowledge will help you on every step of the spiritual path, not least when you embark on a retreat.

The image of who we are becoming is our guide. The retreat is simply part of that process of becoming.

11

A Passion for the Unattainable

The seeking for God is a natural outcome of the maturity of the soul. There is a time in life when a passion is awakened in the soul which gives the soul a longing for the unattainable, and if the soul does not take that direction, then it certainly misses something in life which is its innate longing and in which lies its ultimate satisfaction.   - HAZRAT INAYAT KHAN

Ever since I can remember, I have felt the dull throb of an emotional need that it seemed could never be satisfied.

Nothing could ease the throb. I tried sex, as I suppose everybody does. Sex only worked for a short time. Drugs masked the need but didn't fill it. Coffee didn't do the trick. Cigarettes dulled the throb and covered it over with a smoke screen. I tried science fiction novels. They helped me ignore the throb for the length of time it took to read the novel. Whatever I tried—and remember, I was trying without any conscious idea of what I was really trying to do—failed to fill the aching void that seemed to be in me every waking and possibly every sleeping moment.

When I quit smoking, I felt the throb with renewed vigor. I realized that it was that throb that I had been trying to cover up with the smoking. At first, I thought this redoubled throb was due to nicotine deprivation. But long after the symptoms of nicotine deprivation should have gone away, I still felt the throb in all its power. I realized then that it was a throb that had to do with the human soul, and I started to wonder how many other people were experiencing this same background emotional roaring.

I wondered if the whole human race might not be feeling this throb. And I came to the conclusion that this aching was simply the spiritual yearning of humankind of which all the ecstatic poets speak.

What is the best way I've personally found for dealing with this fundamental longing? I have a two-fold method. I meditate. And I express my creativity by crafting beautiful objects in my workshop.

Hazrat Inayat Khan writes,

> When the light of love has been lit, the heart becomes transparent, so that the intelligence of the soul can see through it; but until the heart is kindled by the flame of love, the intelligence, which is constantly yearning to experience life on the surface, gropes in the dark.

The Limitations of Possessions

There are many different ways of trying to assuage the passion for the unattainable. Not all are satisfactory. One popular   means is by acquiring possessions in whatever form—things, friends, whatever we think we can own—but acquiring possessions is only another of those gropings in the dark that Hazrat Inayat Khan mentions. It's a groping that makes us feel alive, but only temporarily. Possessions do satisfy our longings, but only for a moment.

Hazrat Inayat Khan doesn't say anywhere that giving up possessions helps kindle our heart into a flame of love. The path of the renunciation of worldly goods is encouraged by some, but it is not the Sufi way. Sufism holds that we should awaken within life, not outside it. It declares that our hearts can be on fire with love although we own a nice car—even if it is a Rolls-Royce. The important thing to understand is that the Rolls-Royce, although it is a nice car, is just a car and won't satisfy our yearning to experience being at its fullest.

Having stuff brings fleeting satisfaction but it also brings permanant problems. If you have stuff, you have to pay attention to that stuff. Every day that I go into my cabinetmaker's shop I look around and take a mental inventory of my tools, right down to the drill bits, and I have hundreds of those. This clutters up my mind. My mind is further cluttered by the resentment and disapproval that well up within me each time I take this inventory. I think of the tools I don't have, of the perfect stranger who messed up one I do have, and so on and so forth. When you consider that my shop-inventory resentments are then shoved onto the usual pile of resentments we all have—he done me wrong, she done me wrong, it done me wrong, et cetera, et cetera—you can imagine how totally cluttered my mind really is.

The Coffee Shop That Refused to Be Separate

Sex, smoking, food, drink, having possessions—these are not the only ways we have of temporarily appeasing our yearning for the unattainable. There are a hundred other ways.

You'll recall that on that long retreat I described, I spent fifteen days isolated from the world in a small hut. The main constituents of my diet were granola, apple juice and rice cakes. By the time the retreat was over, I was experiencing a high degree of grease deprivation. I hadn't had a New York Coffee Shop breakfast of meat, eggs and hash browns for fifteen days.

As I was getting into my car, I asked my retreat guide to give me directions to the nearest restaurant that would serve me a good New York-style breakfast. She was at something of a loss. Perhaps, as a vegetarian, she was reluctant to tell me. But she finally came through with a name and a place, and I left at top speed, stopping on the way only to buy *The New York Times*. (I was also suffering from intense *New York Times* Crossword Puzzle deprivation.)

I arrived at the designated restaurant, plunked myself down at the counter, and placed my order in a single breath: "Two poached on hash, potatoes, wheat toast, coffee." The man behind the counter stared at me blankly. I remembered I wasn't in a New York City coffee shop and repeated my order slowly.

Soon my breakfast arrived. This not being New York, it was a compromise—no hash browns and the eggs not poached. But I still set to with a relish.

I was halfway through my breakfast and not quite halfway through my crossword puzzle when a voice came over the public address system. It said: "Ladies and gentlemen, it is now time to say the Pledge of Allegiance to the flag of the United States of America. Will everyone please rise and face the flag?"

My first thought was that my retreat guide had made a mistake and directed me into a parallel universe, one where the U.S. government was a touch more dictatorial. I looked around and saw that if this were a parallel universe, it was an extremely good copy of my own. Furthermore, everybody was standing up. So I did what any sane person would do when confronted with the customs of a foreign country: I stood up, said the Pledge of Allegiance along with everyone else, and sat down again to finish my breakfast. (I didn't finish the crossword puzzle. This was Friday, when they are harder. I had to finish it on a driving break farther along.)

The owner of the coffee shop had found a way to assuage his feelings of separation, his desire for the unattainable. That way was to make everyone join him for a brief moment of union in the recitation of the Pledge of Allegiance.

It wasn't much of a union, really—just a gesture in that direction. But even the regular customers, who had readily fallen in with this ritual to assuage their feelings of separation, had a sense of satisfaction. I could feel it.

The regulars might even have felt satisfyingly smug and defiant. After all, they had had the pleasure of seeing strangers being forced to conform to this well-known but slightly unusual ritual. This was okay with me. We all have moments of smug defiance. Far from being offended, I was charmed. Now, I don't intend to make the Pledge of Allegiance part of my daily meditation routine. But my encounter with patriotism in that small-town coffee shop stirred deeper resonances in me.

No matter how veiled from us the the secrets of the greater cosmos seem to be, we all still feel the need to express our commitment to that greater cosmos. We can't shake the belief that there must be some way of acknowledging our innate belongingness to a whole that is greater than the little world we seem to live in. My friends in that small-town coffee shop had found one way of acknowledging that belongingness.

The Unendingness of the Passion for the Unattainable

Our passion for the unattainable, that aching desire we have to experience that we are part of something greater than ourselves, finds many ways of being assuaged in the world around us. I've said that meditation and the exercise of meaningful creativity (in my case, woodworking) can bring us closer to satisfying this yearning. A number of professional healers, all of them working out there in the real world, come to the Sufi Center that Majida and I direct. There is a chiropractor; there are a couple of physical therapists; there is a polarity therapist; there is a nurse practitioner. There are also a number of accomplished healers who, technically speaking, are not professionals. When I hear these people talking about healing, often I hear them expressing the intense creative joy they sometimes experience as they heal others. They talk about practicing healing just like I talk about making furniture. All of us know we are having a meaningful impact on our environment. All of us know this, and that knowledge makes us joyful.

I have already cited the following passage from the writings of Hazrat Inayat Khan, but it takes on added meaning in this context.

> The seeking for God is a natural outcome of the maturity of the soul. There is a time in life when a passion is awakened in the soul which gives the soul a longing for the unattainable, and if the soul does not take that direction, then it certainly misses something in life which is its innate longing and in which lies its ultimate satisfaction . . . . We are born with the thinking of the whole universe, but as our consciousness becomes limited to what we think we are as an individual, we lose the thinking of the universe and base our knowledge upon our experience, or upon our way of interpreting experience. When we rediscover that thinking, we realize how inadequate our personal thinking is.

There is no end to our yearning for the unattainable, not even for the best of us. Once, when I was driving the Pir to Kennedy Airport, he suddenly said to me, "I'm 75 years old and only now am I understanding what it means to be a Sufi." I wasn't quite sure how to respond to this unexpected announcement, and I said nothing. But the Pir's admission told me a lot about spiritual progress. My own breakthroughs come at ten-year intervals—or so it seems, maybe because each one of them is so exhausting that it takes me nine years to work up the courage to try for another breakthrough. Or maybe it just seems that way; maybe the intervals are a whole lot shorter. The fact is that we need only look at how attached we all are to— well, to just about everything—to understand why the intervals between revelations are so long. (You'll be able to accept this as a fact only if you are a mature seeker.)

EXERCISE 13: *Being Greater*

This practice demands that we be continually aware of the limitations of our experience and the probability that there is other, as yet undiscovered, territory waiting to open itself before us.

For the next minute or so, try to imagine that what you know is bigger than you know. If you honestly try to do this, you will experience a sort of psychic stretching. Do you remember when you were a kid and you tried to blow up a new balloon, and right at the start it seemed like it would be impossible to blow it up? When you feel a psychic stretching and feel like you can't stretch any more, think of that balloon—and then relax into the exercise and allow the soul's desire to take shape. How do you do this? You can facilitate the process of allowing by calmly remembering that who the world says you are is only a tiny portion of your being. Remember, too, that "up" and "out," and all those other words, are merely words. Everything that is, is there within you.

Sometimes when I explain what I've just explained, a student exclaims, "I never imagined that God was unattainable!" I'm not saying God is unattainable. When we talk about the passion for the unattainable, we are referring to that state in which we have an intimation of the actual vastness of creation. This is not an intellectual or philosophical experience, but a direct perception of reality, a perception that every mystical order knows about and seeks. What I've been trying to do is point to the existence of this experience. I can't really describe it. As is so often true in the world of the mystics, words are useless when we talk about perceiving in this way. All we can really do is talk around the subject.

People from the East are less likely to think that just because they expend effort, they will get something. They are more likely to trust the word of the teacher and believe that expending the effort is enough in itself. A passion for the unobtainable seems perfectly normal in the East, where it is seen as God's testing of God's own limits. (Our psyche has to translate this into its own personal terms for us to understand it at all.) Hazrat Inayat Khan writes:

> To the Sufi, the soul is a current that joins the physical body to the source. And the art of repose naturally makes it easier for the soul to experience freedom, inspiration, power, because it is then loosened from the grip of the physical body. As Rumi says in the *Masnavi*, "Man is a captive on earth. His body and his mind are his prison bars. And the soul is unconsciously craving to experience once again the freedom which originally belonged to it." The Platonic idea about reaching the higher source is the same: that by exaltation the soul, so to speak, rises above the fast hold of the physical body; it may be only for a few moments, but it experiences in those moments a freedom which man has never experienced before.
>
> A moment of exaltation is a different experience at every level. The supreme exaltation is hinted at in the Bible: "Be ye perfect even as your Father in heaven is perfect." Many religious people will say that it is impossible for man to be perfect; but it is said in the Bible just the same. At all times the knowers and seers have understood that there is a stage at which, by touching a particular phase of existence, one feels raised above the limitations of life, and is given that power and peace and freedom, that light and life, which belong to the source of all beings. In other words, in that moment of supreme exaltation one is not only united with the source of all beings, but dissolved in it; for the source is one's self.

This is heady territory; we are talking about the unattainable. When I first started looking into the spiritual life, I thought the sorts of experiences Murshid described were just around the corner. All I had to do to have them was express a desire, meditate for twenty minutes or so, and bingo, there I was. Now I know better. But these kinds of experiences, difficult as they are to achieve, are absolutely within our grasp. Note that Hazrat Inayat Khan quotes, as he did in many of his lectures, from the Bible: "Be ye perfect even as your Father in Heaven is perfect." Murshid used this quotation in many contexts, but his meaning was always the same: perfection is actually attainable, and its attainment should be our objective. We can revisit the state to which Rumi refers when he says in the *Masnavi*: "The soul is unconsciously craving to experience once again the freedom which originally belonged to it."

The Unveiling of New Universes

Think about it. For some reason that you cannot remember, you, or whatever it is that presently identifies itself as you, deliberately decided to give up freedom in order to put on the fetters of physical existence. Why would anyone want to do this? The classic answer of the mystics is that in experiencing freedom within limitations, we break the bonds of conventional creation and force new universes to unveil themselves. We demand that our beings allow what is unknown but possible to express itself within us, even though that seems impossible. What comes may look to our limited minds like a totally altered reality, even though it was really already there. The difficulty is that we tend to concentrate on our limitations, believing they are us. But we are not our limitations. We are that aspect of the divine engaged in resolving the paradox, or, as Pir Vilayat constantly put it, "reconciling the irreconcilables."

Once we have been born on earth, a fascinating thing happens. Despite our feelings of desperation and separation, we genuinely begin to feel a passion for the unattainable. When we recognize that above all else we are driven to fulfill it, we submit ourselves to a spiritual discipline and begin to realize that our limitations are not us. This is exciting—or it can be and it should be—because knowing our personal limitations and our broader human and physical reality-based limitations allows us to ignore and step outside these limitations, even if only for a nanosecond. Thus we are able to turn reality on its head and experience God experiencing creation.

Once you have done this, nothing is ever the same again. You have discovered that you are not alone.

"A passion for the unattainable" is only a metaphysical way of saying that all the universes, all the various planes of existence, finally constitute a very big place. But we human beings can own a great deal of that very big place. We can't have it all; there is too much, and some areas are restricted to particular beings (just trust me on this one). But we can have a lot.

What is equally interesting is that no two people carry exactly the same items into the universe. We each bring a little something unique to ourselves. Let's think of creation as a kind of spiral. Human evolution appears repetitive and circular, but it is really always advancing upward. Within the spiral, each person contributes something. The complex interplay of all our contributions creates an amazingly balanced energy form—or it can.

This actually works only when everyone links up. At the animalistic level, this linking energy forms a mob. At the angelic level, it creates the music of the spheres.

Most of us are stuck somewhere in between, sounding our plaintive individual notes and hoping someone will harmonize with us. Hang out with the Sufis long enough, and you'll eventually hear them say in one way or another that not only do they want you to sing well, but they want you to sing right out to the limit of your capabilities. And that limit is always going to stretch much further than you think.

12

Love

The heart that is free of love sickness isn't a heart at all. The body deprived of the pangs of love is nothing but clay and water.

- JAMI

There are three kinds of love. The first is love in the marketplace. Here we bargain with our partner. We say, "Love me, and I might reciprocate," or, "I love you, and I demand that you reciprocate." The second is the love that sees others as beings to be tolerated with quirks that perhaps we accept. This is better than the first kind of love. The third is that love that sees all others as part and parcel of Allah. This is the best kind of love. It can't be faked. It is the Sufi kind of love.

The Value of Vulnerability

At the personal level, trust is an essential component of love. You have to give your trust to someone in such a way that, when it comes to the other person, you are vulnerable. Pir-o-Murshid writes,

> He who guards himself against being fooled by another is clever; he who does not allow another to fool him is wise; he who is fooled by another is a simpleton; but he who knowingly allows himself to be fooled shows the character of the saint.

An old friend of mine once did her best to convince me that we have to be in a state of total vulnerability when we encounter someone else. She felt that only then did we have a chance of penetrating through to the real nature of that person.

She understood, of course, that when you act in this way you risk rebuff. She felt, though, that the risk was well worth taking. In her view, being rebuffed was an acceptable price to pay for the rewards that can come our way if we maintain this state of vulnerability.

Such was my friend's assertion. At first I wasn't happy with what she said and disagreed with her. As we went on talking, though, I realized that what I wasn't happy with was the possibility of humiliation. Imagine seeing someone you're fairly certain has nothing in common with you. Maybe it's someone you think doesn't like you, or someone who seems to feel a lofty sense of superiority to you and would rather just ignore you. Now, imagine going up to that person and saying, "Let's talk!"

Probably when you picture yourself doing this and imagine what the results might be, you find yourself saying, "Love may be universal, but I think I'll let somebody else work with this person." At least, that was my initial reaction to what my friend was saying.

But, as the discussion continued, I realized that what she was proposing was what I do anyway. I haven't approached people who make me feel totally alienated, but I have approached people in a spirit of curiosity or maybe just because I'd never gotten to know them and felt I should. I once approached someone who flat-out told me she couldn't think of a single reason why we should talk. That was very embarrassing—but I got over it. I think my friend who advocates total vulnerability is right: Vulnerability is the key to trust. And trust is the key to love.

I'm not saying that you should deliberately seek out someone you don't like and make a huge effort to understand that person. Wait—maybe I am saying that, but I don't want to passionately encourage you to do this. I just want to point out that often the greatest barrier to any kind of interpersonal communication—the reason that we have trouble feeling comfortable with another person—is that we are unwilling to be vulnerable.

Being vulnerable is the key to spirituality. You don't progress by knowing. You progress by surrendering your intellectual knowledge. In so doing, you create a vacuum, a vulnerability that God can take advantage of by filling you with divinely inspired curiosity and, ultimately, awareness.

Maybe God sees it like this: When you become vulnerable, you create a space that allows someone else to participate in your experience. And these personal accommodations open us out to higher levels of accommodation.

Meditation is a state of emotional and spiritual vulnerability. In meditating, you open yourself out to whatever (or whomever—the Beloved?) comes along. You accommodate yourself to the possibility of responding to God's intentions on the world's stage. (Still, don't automatically assume that you are actively responding. Just know that the possibility is there!) Meditation has many purposes. One purpose to to create a vulnerability to the spirit of the Beloved. On this personal level, the approach of the Beloved is really about your own soul's coming closer.

I haven't heard the phrase for a while, but is that talk about "soul mates" still making the rounds? When I hear the term "soul mate," I always think, "What, only one?" As if in this whole wide universe there were only one soul that resonates perfectly with yours! I believe it isn't the idea of having a soul mate that appeals to us, but the idea of being rescued. Rescued from what? For one thing, from the annoying need to be vulnerable and therefore risk the even more annoying experience of being humiliated.

Love is not about finding a soul mate. (If it seems to be at the beginning, the feeling that you have found yours starts to dissipate once you and your soul mate discover how different your toothpaste habits are.) Love is about exploring vulnerability. Love prompts us to explore the degree to which we can resist and accept one another. On the spiritual level, love is about continually reaching out for deeper and deeper levels of trust in God.

EXERCISE 14: *Entering the Soul of Another*

Choose a person you would like to understand better. You can choose an acquaintance, a friend, a relative—even your teacher, if you are in a spiritual group. Imagine that that person is in front of you. Imagine gradually entering into that other person's body, getting inside that other person's skin.

Enter into the thoughts of that person. Imagine how that person thinks. Try to get behind the thoughts to the deeper motivations.

That is the first step. Getting beyond the skin is difficult. The closer you are, the harder it is to know what a person is really like. The way you see that person is wrapped up in the way you see the relationship and the way you see yourself. For purposes of this exercise, it might be helpful for you to pretend your knowledge of that person is incorrect or at least incomplete. There are a good many things you don't know, and your object in this exercise is to find out what some of those things are.

Now try to imagine that that person is as fully realized as she or he can possibly be. The key is to think of that person independently of your mutual relationship, not in terms of the relationship he or she has with you. Don't think of the way you want this person to be. Think of how your friend (or relative or teacher) could be in light of her or his potential—how she or he really is. As you do this, desire with all your heart that this person realize his or her completeness. Simultaneously, bear in mind that this completeness may or may not include you, and that either alternative is okay.

It helps to see the person as surrounded by white light, as totally pure, totally without guile, completely innocent yet spiritually mature.

This practice is intended to give you an insight you might not otherwise have into the other person. It is also meant to create an accommodation for the transformation of each of you. You're dedicating a portion of your psychic support to that person. He or she is free to accept or reject that support, but it can only be rejected—or accepted—if it is offered.

Vulnerability can be periodic. Think of total vulnerability as an ideal state, not one you have to be in every moment. Our psyches are delicate; regard vulnerability as a flower that opens, then closes for a bit to renew its energy.

Hazrat Inayat Khan writes,

> Enter unhesitatingly, Beloved, for in this abode there is naught but my longing for Thee. Do I call Thee my soul? But Thou art my spirit. Can I call Thee my life? But Thou livest forever. May I call Thee my Beloved? But Thou art Love itself. Then what must I call Thee? I must call Thee myself.

Our natural state, that from which we spring, is pure and innocent. In our natural state, we know ourselves as an essence—maybe THE essence—of divine love. Then we are born, and we forget. That doesn't mean love has deserted us. It's still there; we've just forgotten about it. The call from within is a reminder: "Hey, remember me?"

Divine love seems alien to us because it is so different from what we have grown to accept. Our coming into physical reality engenders in us mistaken assumptions about love. Vulnerability allows us to recognize that it is these mistaken assumptions that are alien.

Once we've realized at least a part of this truth, we have the responsibility of further accommodating divine love within our earthly beings. We have the responsibility of joining in the effort of all humanity to evolve further within the confines of our limited existence.

Love as Wadud: *The Feeling That Created the Universe*

One word that the Sufis use for love is one of the names of God, the attribute *Wadud*. It was out of Wadud that God created the universe. Pir Vilayat, paraphrasing Ibn

'Arabi, liked to say that God created the universe by "fragmenting Himself," by descending from the solitude of peace. Why? Simply out of His love for the possibility of me and you, Pir Vilayat explained, out of his love for the possibility of every single object in the universe.

Imagine the quality of the energy that expresses itself by creating the immense vastnesses of the many planes of existence solely for the love of the possibility of you and me. Doesn't that make you feel better about your life?

Wadud is one of the divine qualities of God, those qualities that the Sufis term *Sifat*. We call into manifestation in ourselves the same divine love that engendered creation. Part of this process consists in remembering and repeating the word Wadud. By repeating this word we concentrate on the divine archetype of Wadud, Wadud as manifested in God. Our concentration helps bring this quality down to earth, incarnating it within our individual beings. Such calling into manifestation is difficult, to say the least. We must repeat the word Wadud with a mastery of every subtlety of the unique vibrations that its syllables embody.

Love as Ishq: *Divine Nostalgia*

Wadud is the word for divine love that Sufis most commonly use. Pir-o-Murshid, though, preferred another word: *Ishq*. Ishq is love and intense desire, a nostalgia for the divine. Ishq is the longing we all experience at a very deep level, often not knowing exactly what the object of this longing is. Ishq is a yearning to be reunited with the Beloved, even in our uncertainty about who the Beloved is. Ishq is an elusive sense of incompleteness that can be remedied only by communion with an undefined aspect of ourselves that is somehow difficult to connect with or even understand. Such is the meaning of *Ishq*—at least as I currently understand it. Pir Vilayat writes,

> Is love pleasure, is love merriment? No, love is longing constantly; love is persevering unweariedly; love is hoping patiently; love is willing surrender; love is regarding constantly the pleasure and displeasure of the Beloved, for love is resignation to the will of the possessor of one's heart; it is love that teaches man: "Thou, not I."

This description of divine love may strike you as mawkish and maudlin. You may even feel inclined to ask, "Are all Sufis just lovesick adolescents?"

What we have to remember is that Pir Vilayat, and his father, and the long line of Sufi seers that came before them, speak from a very lofty level. Like eagles, they have soared into the sky. Like the highest-flying of all birds, they can settle on mountaintops that no one else can reach. It is from this vantage-point that they survey the cosmos and speak to us of the true nature of divine love.

You and I are not yet that eagle on the mountaintop. When the seers speak to us from high above the level we have presently achieved, we should at least give them the benefit of the doubt by listening.

Perhaps, as you repeat Wadud and continue to reach for the divine impulse of love that gave birth to the created universe, you will begin to get a glimmering of what the ancient prophets and modern pirs mean. Let us set aside for a moment the lofty goal of reaching the mountaintop. Perhaps we will at least be able to move beyond personal emotion to cosmic emotion. You can't

bring about this sort of shift in your soul if all you're thinking about is whether somebody loves you. Pir Vilayat constantly exhorted us to get into the thinking of the universe, to experience the greater manifestation of God's
existence. Love is a part of that, and once we begin to
truly grasp this higher thinking of the universe, all these
lesser manifestations of love will appear less important (and
more poignant). Here is an exercise intended to help you
soar to the mountaintop.

EXERCISE 15: *The Flight of the Eagle*

*Put yourself into a state of relaxation. Keep your spine straight,
however. There should be enough tension in your muscles to keep you
completely erect; the rest of you can be completely relaxed.*

*Imagine for a moment that all your knowledge of yourself has
temporarily vanished. Think of yourself as a blank slate, an innocent. It will help you to try to imagine the state you were in when you
were a small child. Try to remember what it was like to be totally
involved in a new experience, completely engrossed by whatever happened to be in front of you (perhaps something that would seem silly
to you as an adult).*

*Can you recall that state? Use any method you can to reproduce
it. The idea is to withdraw from your personality for just a few
moments and imagine that you possess an eagle's vision of the world—
the vision of a lofty eagle, uninvolved in self. If you could actually
become the eagle, how would your personality shift from its normal
perspective? Look at the world from the mountaintop, or from the
loftiness of the eagle's soaring flight. Try to detect what keeps you
from seeing in this way. See if you can discover how you would have
to change to soar or to alight on the mountaintop.*

It has always fascinated me that the Sufi mystics use "love" as the reason behind existence. It has occurred to me to wonder whether it lies beneath the various meanings of "love" today.

Hazrat Inayat Khan writes, "My heart has become an ocean, Beloved, since Thou hast poured Thy love into it."

Is there, in every form of love that exists today—even the most banal—a touch of the divine intention?

13

The Light of Knighthood

Can you imagine taking a vow to become a knight of light as part
of your spiritual practice? The work would entail protecting the
victims of manipulation and greed; in addition, you would act to
counter the actions of those who cause suffering to others. . . .
The only weapons that are permissable in this cosmic crusade are
lances of light that dispel the darkness. In fact, the fulfillment of
such a task requires of us that we awaken the light even in our
own bodies.   - VILAYAT INAYAT KHAN

In the 1830s, the Russian Empire decided to increase its
tax base by annexing numerous peasant villages in the
Caucasus mountains. The Tsar appointed General
Yermoloff, often called "Russia's Wellington," to oversee
the task.

Historian Paul Johnson says Yermoloff's conduct was
"so ferocious that the natives were always in revolt. His
'victories' were successive 'punishments' of 'rebellions' which
were themselves the product of earlier 'victories.'" In Sep-
tember 1819, Yermoloff surrounded the large village of

Dadi-Yourt with six companies of Russian soldiers, seven hundred Cossacks and six pieces of artillery. Twenty-four hours later, the only villagers left alive were fourteen men, all wounded, and one hundred and forty women and children, all prisoners and many also wounded.

The brutal reprisal provoked an internal holy war. The great resistance fighter Shamil, a Naqshbandi Sufi sheikh, led this spiritual war. With equal measures of religious fervor and political pragmatism he cajoled and coerced his fellow Caucasians into fighting the Russians. Most of these men were cast in the fighting mold you would expect from proud, independent mountain tribesmen. Others, including Shamil's own Sufi teacher, were pacifists who refused to carry weapons.

Still, the two kinds of Sufis accepted and supported each other. But by the end of the 1850s the Russians had worn Shamil's warriors down. The Russians had more men and more materiel, and were willing to accept appalling losses.

But it took them thirty years to achieve victory.

Over one hundred and forty years later, the descendants of these same Naqshbandi Sufis took their country back from the crumbling Soviet empire. That country is called Chechnya.

Of course, the Naqshbandis are renowned for being politically active. Our own heritage, the Chistis, has been very different, refraining from political activism and often from political involvement. I've told this story only to illustrate that pacifism isn't necessarily a Sufi quality. We tend to think that warrior-priests should fight only battles of the soul. But it seems that God sometimes has a different task in mind for the Sufi: direct physical combat.

The Russian writer Leo Tolstoy (1828-1910), author of *War and Peace* and *Anna Karenina*, served as an artillery officer in the war against Shamil in 1852, when Tolstoy was twenty-four. In 1896-1904, when he was in his seventies, the great Russian author wrote a short novel, *Hadji Murad*, based on that war. Some critics think *Hadji Murad* is the greatest work of short fiction ever written. The story is really about Shamil's most effective military subordinate, Hadji Murad. But those interested should know that in this novel Tolstoy also paints, with a few subtle and powerful brushstrokes, the character of Shamil himself.

Was Shamil right to wage war?

In the light of today's bloody conflict between Russia and Chechnya, we might think not. But I believe we are too far removed from events to judge. Compared to the inhabitants of the Caucasus in the nineteenth century, we are relatively safe here in the U.S., unlikely to face what Shamil faced. But his story demonstrates that the Sufi knight is a knight in the "real world." Sufi mystics need to know as much as they can about every aspect of the human condition.

If we wish to explore this aspect of the Sufi light of knighthood—that is, the Sufi as warrior-priest in the world—we first have to examine the relationship between the two states of being that the Sufis call *Wahid* and *Ahid,* Multiplicity in Unity and Unity in Multiplicity.

To properly explore the relationship between these two states, we must try to understand the state that the Sufis call *Zat* in Persian and *Dhat* in Arabic, and which underlies *Wahid* and *Ahid*. (Pir-o-Murshid, coming from a Persian/Urdu background, used the Persian spelling "Zat," which has the advantage of being pronounceable by English speakers. I'll confine myself to this spelling.)

In seeking to understand these states of being, we are seeking to understand no less than the nature of God! It is good to be mindful of the words of the tenth-century Sufi master Al-Hujwiri in the *Kashf Al-Mahjub* (*Revelation of the Mystery*): "Knowledge of Him is attained only by unceasing bewilderment of the reason, and His favor is not procured by any act of human acquisition but is miraculously revealed to men's hearts."

Zat: *The Ground of All Being.*

Zat is the undifferentiated, uncreated, solitary place, the unique, pre-creation state of God, from which all being issues. Sufi metaphysicians believe that at the moment when God made the decision to manifest, to express His/Her love of possibility, Zat contracted. Part of its essence coalesced into *Nur*, the light of creation and the all-pervading light of the physical universe. (An-Nur is also one of the 99 Names of God.)

International Relations Professor Dr. Abdul Aziz Said, who occupies the endowed Saeed Farsee Chair of Islamic Peace at American University, Washington, D.C., and is himself a Sufi sheikh, describes the state of Zat as follows (I am paraphrasing):

Imagine that you are deep in the desert. It is late at night. You are far from civilization, far from any source of artificial illumination. The sky is overcast; there is no moon and the light of the stars is not visible. It is as dark as a coal mine two miles beneath the surface of the earth.

Within this darkness, you have made a campfire. The campfire gives off a flickering light. Imagine that this campfire, and the light it gives off for as far into the wilderness as it can penetrate, is all of the universes, all creation, all of the created planes of existence.

Zat is all that which is beyond this circle of light. It is the unchanging essence that creates and yet is unaffected by creation. It is the endless darkness beyond the campfire's light that has given birth to the campfire.

This place, this Zat, is also the "solitude of peace" from which God, fragmenting Him/Herself, created the physical universe.

How do we know that Zat is as I've described it? Some of the great Sufi sages seem to have directly experienced this state. Some of them have left us descriptions. Nevertheless, Zat is, as Al-Hujwiri states so eloquently, quite beyond the reach of human reason.

Out of Nur: The Ninety-Nine Names of God

When Zat contracted and creation came into existence, a variety of attributes formed within Nur or the uncreated all-pervading light of the cosmos. Two of them were the all-important states of Wahid, Multiplicity in Unity, and Ahid, Unity in Multiplicity, which I have already mentioned.

The attributes in general are indicative of Sifat, that is, the Ninety-Nine Names of God (the names have been exported from Islam). Over the centuries, the Sufis have added words such as An-Nur and *Al-Quddus*, the latter denoting "The Most Pure," "The Unblemished," "The Holiest" (see Notes).

Pir Vilayat used to tell us that in Ahid—in Unity in Multiplicity—all things, including energies and bodies, form a single energy field, one without boundaries and one which pulsates within Zat.

On the other hand, Multiplicity in Unity, or Wahid, consists of an infinity of discrete entities. It is the expression of the trillions upon trillions of dust motes that make up individuated consciousnesses and all other separate entities in the universe—chairs, tables, elements, planets, stars, and so on.

The Sufi knight is conscious of unity. Therefore, she or he can fearlessly carry out actions within the multiplicity.

Was the Sufi warrior Shamil in this state?

Perhaps.

If you read Leo Tolstoy's short novel *Hadji Murad*, you will see that perhaps Hadji Murad was in this state as well.

It seems that the one and the many lie in a state of equanimity within the Sufi knight. This Sufi knight, while not a member of an elite, cherishes a high degree of honor—honor that has to do with the Self, not with the personality. Hazrat Inayat Khan writes the following.

> For a Sufi the sense of honor is not for his personality, he does not give his person a greater place than dust and the central theme of his life is simplicity and his moral is humility. Yet remember that the Sufi breathes the breath of God, so he is conscious of the honor of God. His pride is greater, therefore, than the pride of every man. It is in the intoxication of this pride that he proves to be God-conscious.

Here is an exercise that will help you to find the Sufi warrior-priest within yourself.

EXERCISE 16: *Imagining the Knight*

In this exercise, create a mental picture of a knight from your imagination. Use everything that you have ever heard or read about knights, reaching as far inside yourself as you can.

Don't worry about whether the image is historically accurate. Shamil is an example of the warrior-knight. But you might just as well choose the Samurai warrior-knights of ancient Japan. Accounts tell us that a Samurai warrior was totally still and completely at peace—until the moment of conflict came, when his state was transformed into total action.

For this exercise you need to conjure up mind images of the ideal rather than of living breathing human beings. Try to imagine what the ideal state of knighthood is like. You can never live up to such an ideal, because that is just what it is—an ideal. But the point is not to replicate reality exactly. The point is to actually participate, to the extent that it is possible for you, in the experience of knighthood, not just look on.

When you have sifted through some of these images and begun to grasp their essence, it might help you to imagine, if only for a moment, that you are fearless. Imagine that for the purposes of this exercise only! If you owe the Mafia $10,000 and the collectors are threatening to break your legs, you are not going to be able to solve this problem simply by imagining that you are fearless. This exercise is not meant to help you solve the ordinary problems of everyday life. No; I am simply asking you to try for a moment to feel what it is like to be fearless.

Now, try to imagine that God is being fearless through you. If you'd rather not try this, at least try to imagine that you're in a state of fearlessness. You are the fearless one, but that fearlessness is also God's fearlessness manifesting through you.

Remember that the Sufi knight participates in the divine at-tributes of Wahid—Multiplicity in Unity—and Ahid—Unity in Multiplicity. Try to imagine these two attributes of the divine as manifesting through you.

Now try to imagine that what the Sufis call Qahr—*Divine Sovereignty—is manifesting within you. What would it feel like to have personal access in your being to this quality? I am not telling you that you do indeed have personal access to this quality; I am asking you to try to feel what it would be like to have that personal access.*

A key ingredient to successfully carrying out these exercises is what Pir-o-Murshid called "the art of repose." The art of repose is one of the keys to God-Realization.

It is remarkably difficult to relax, to be in that state of total relaxation where none of our muscles is tense and our mind and emotions are on standby, simply doing nothing. That is the place where you have to be to know the mind of the knight, of the warrior-priest.

EXERCISE 17: *The Art of Repose*

Practice relaxation for the next two or three days. Let go of any preconceptions you may have about what constitutes the spiritual life. Let go of any notion you may have that a spiritual person is superior or a member of an elite. Slip back into the arms of the Trusted One—Him or Her whom I have been calling the Beloved—and simply empty your mind. See what comes. Let what comes, come, remembering to let go of all of your presuppositions about what is to come. Maybe nothing will come. In which case, that is what comes. In that case, nothing is good.

In his public sessions, Pir Vilayat was in the habit of asking us to get down on one knee, as if we were medieval knights in a sacred sanctuary vowing allegiance to a sovereign. He asked us to think, "I will," and repeat Fatah—*"the Opener"—several times while doing so. Fatah is that one of the Ninety-Nine Names of God that refers to the opening of the heart. It is the outward expansion of our being in the service of and devotion to God that Sufism calls for. Fatah is also used as an affirmation of other spiritual vows; it is not uncommon to recite it thirty-three times at the end of a personal retreat.*

Have you been able to slip back into the arms of the Trusted One and empty your mind a little? If so, try to stretch yourself a bit more by imagining what it would be like not to have to think about doing this at all, but just to be it. Begin to imagine that state now, because it will take you a very long time to be able to realize it.

When I started out as a carpenter, too many years ago, the man I was working for told me it would take me two years to learn to use a hammer. I didn't believe him. After all, the hammer is a simple tool, right? Two years later, almost to the day, I suddenly realized I was fastening two-by-fours together without thinking about the hammer. I was just doing it. But it had taken me the whole two years.

You must never come to think, in pursuing the spiritual path, that there are things that simply can't be done at all. The mistaken personal belief that something can't be done is the first and greatest barrier to self-realization. Get over that and get back to doing your practice; there will come a day when the doing of it is so automatic that all you need to do is just be. Begin now to practice having access to the archetype of the knight. Once you've acquired that access, the archetype will come in very handy.

With regard, once more, to Ibn 'Arabi's description of God's fragmenting Him/Herself to create the physical universe: it is the word "fragmenting" that is key here. Within the blazing uncreated light of pure love, something was missing—or maybe nothing was missing and creation just happened, or maybe it just seemed like a good idea at the time, or maybe something else entirely was involved. The point is that there was creation, and here we are, the results of that fragmentation, trying once more to attain that uncreated light that we dimly sense even while we are not at all sure about its nature. But we struggle on, because Sufism tells us in its very subtle way that what we suppose to be real is not real at all, and that what is truly real is hidden from us, veiled. We are also told that beneath the veils, inside the hidden rooms, there is a state of light-filled ecstasy that has created out of itself a new being—you!— and knows its power and purpose. You, as part of this, can know that power and purpose as well.

Sound good? How do you get some? Mevlana Jalaluddin Rumi provides a clue.

Remember the deep root of your being, the presence of your lord. Give your life to the one who already owns your breath and your moments. If you don't, you will be exactly like the man who takes a precious dagger and hammers it into his kitchen wall for a peg to hold his dipper gourd. You'll be wasting valuable keenness and foolishly ignoring your dignity and your purpose.

EXERCISE 18: *You Are a Being of Light (II)*

Imagine that you are a Being of Light. Imagine that you are much greater than your physical body, expanding on the out-breath as far as you can imagine and contracting on the in-breath to just beyond the limits of your physical body. Keep this practice simple, and if you are able to keep your imagination focused for that length of time, do it for at least five minutes. What I mean by keep it simple is that if any other phenomena, such as inner lights or sounds, intrude, stop and start over again.

Our personalities are convinced that they are isolated. It doesn't seem to matter how many extraordinary experiences we have; there is still a part of us, the larger part most likely, that experiences itself as isolated and alone. It isn't until we actually begin to experience the reality of our "light-beingness," and its commingling with the light-beingness of other people, that we are less burdened by loneliness. Even when we do experience this, our personality does not automatically let go of its negative commentaries. The personality needs to be prodded; it needs to be persuaded and stroked before it will allow itself to be changed.

It is good and proper to ask your spiritual guide for advice about these matters. We have been talking about the Sufi knight of light. In the age of chivalry, the more experienced knights trained the less experienced, or at least acted as role models. On the Sufi path as in similar spiritual pursuits, the more experienced guide takes on and trains the less experienced student. The person with the greater access to the capability of knighthood offers that access to the student.

Ultimately, of course, our loyalty, trust and service are to be offered to God. I'm not speaking here about blind faith, the robotic acceptance of whatever we fearfully think must be the will of God. Those who know their duty, their purpose, their place, are also aware of their whole being; they know that they co-create with the entire universe. It is, to say the least, empowering to know this; suddenly, you are bigger. Stay with that bigness. Become the knight of illumination that you are.

14

Sacrifice

"What sense is there, O moth, in burning yourself in trying to kiss the light?" "My joy in it is greater than my sacrifice."
                                        - HAZRAT INAYAT KHAN

There is a group within the Sufi Order called Ziraat. *Ziraat* is the Persian (Farsi) word for farming or agriculture. As used by the Ziraat group, *ziraat* means spiritual farming.

Spiritual farming is the same as earthly agriculture in that in spiritual farming you also have to plow up the ground before you plant again. And, just like real farming, everything has to be plowed up, every bit of old growth, even if it looks like it might still have some value. It all has to be discarded so that new growth—the growth of the spirit— can take place.

When we pursue the spiritual path and discover that old growth has to be discarded, we find this scary. Maybe we'll have to sacrifice something we love!

It wasn't until I suddenly had a spate of apprehensive queries that I realized how much my students worried about this "plowing up." One student was afraid she might have to give up her acting career. Another was worried she would lose the desire to create that was turning her into an accomplished woodworker. And so on.

And it's a concern. But, when the process begins, you may find yourself sacrificing something you think you love and discovering that what you're sacrificing isn't what you thought it was at all.

This happened to me. At the beginning of my spiritual career, I abruptly gave up something I dearly loved—or thought I did.

I'm a competent chess player, certainly not world-class but above the level of the average wood-pusher. One afternoon in the early days of my stay at the Khanaqa as-Safiya in New York, I was sitting in the lounge playing a game of chess with a fellow Sufi student when the director walked by (I won't reveal her name). As she passed she glanced down at the board and muttered a single word. It sounded like "competition."

That word—whether she said it or whether I just thought I heard it—galvanized me into action. From that moment I couldn't play chess any more. I gave away all my chess books. While I was doing this I realized that it wasn't chess I was sacrificing. What I was giving up was my need to be successfully competitive. It was this need that had kept me at the game and made me think I enjoyed chess much more than I did.

But from that time on I've no longer had the need to compete successfully. So I didn't sacrifice chess (in which I quickly lost interest); I sacrificed my need to compete successfully.

I've noticed that people who've been on the spiritual path for some time rarely have hobbies or obsessive pastimes. They usually aren't collectors or sports fans. They consider their lives to be important. They don't have much room in them for pastime clutter.

The Last Class

When you pursue the path you sometimes find yourself compelled to give up something you didn't particularly like in the first place but felt you couldn't give up for practical reasons. I had an older student who taught English Composition and Literature for many years, sometimes full-time, sometimes part-time, here, there, and everywhere. He'd never liked teaching and did it to support his family (he was engaged in other pursuits as well, such as writing, which are notorious for their inability to bring in money). Though he had this aversion to teaching, my student had always been successful and popular as a teacher.

But he set out along the Sufi path, almost off-handedly, and then one night, a month into the term, he stood in front of a class of students and couldn't think of a thing to say. He cancelled the class. The same thing happened at the next class—and the next. The week after that, he resigned. He never returned to teaching.

This was not a wonderful experience for him. He was greatly distressed. It wasn't until a month after he'd quit teaching that he realized what had happened—or at least began to realize. His steadily evolving inner self couldn't fake teaching anymore. It had compelled him to be true, or truer, to who he really was.

Shifts in perception can emerge in unexpected, impractical ways. It's easy to fool ourselves about these changes. Progressing along the Sufi path is a subtle process, sometimes almost a dangerous one. In cases such as that of my English-teaching student, it's best to consult a spiritual guide.

Self-Change and Relationship Change

When you embark on the path, there is one category of "stuff" in particular that seems to get sacrificed early on. You may find that you have to sacrifice the relationships you accumulated to support whatever old assumptions you had about yourself.

Your friends will be disturbed when they discover you're reconsidering how you fit into the world. Those who are used to your acting in a certain way may be upset to see you expand, become softer and more flexible. They'll do their best to get you back to where you were before. The struggle can become serious, especially because at first you and your friends may not understand what's happening.

Let's suppose that before you entered on the spiritual path you expended a lot of creative energy talking about baseball. You and your friends argued statistics and the merits of players. Your emotions were bound up with the fortunes of a particular team.

Then you found meditation. Your thoughts moved in new directions. Baseball began to seem trivial.

There's no way this won't upset your friends who depend on you to talk baseball with them. The layer of humanity to which you were attached no longer works for you. To extricate yourself from this layer is going to be a delicate business. You may have to pretend interest while weaning your friends from your presence.

All of this becomes especially problematical when the friend in question is your spouse.

The changes in you, the shifts that take place, are gradual. To the person in whom they're taking place—you—they may seem colossal. You may tend to exaggerate them. In particular, you may tend to exaggerate them in your relationship with your partner. Even when you don't exaggerate them, your spouse may have trouble accepting them. Then you need to be as honest with your partner as you can. Tell him or her that you have this spiritual work to do and you would be happy for simple emotional support.

You're not asking your partner to participate. You're asking him or her to be patient. However, if your partner tries to slow your progress down—usually unconsciously— you will have to be patient yourself. This slowing-down of your progress can take the form of a variety of subtle undermining moves. Your partner may even believe he or she is actually being supportive.

Then again, you may be in for a big surprise. You may discover that your partner or significant other or long-time companion is quite willing to support you. Whether it's one or the other doesn't seem to depend on any single factor, except perhaps the degree of self-confidence of the partner. But when you're shifting from one level of relationship to another, especially in a marriage, there is bound to be friction, and you will have to think carefully about what you're willing to sacrifice. My advice has always been that unless there is actual abuse of some sort, there's always a way to sort things out.

Perhaps it's wrong to speak of a shift from one level of relationship to another. Perhaps it's more accurate to say that we acquire a broader view of reality, that our perception of reality expands. When this first begins to affect our relationships, it can be devastating. We seem to be losing friends one after the other. To compound our anxieties, often (particularly in the early stages, and because of our lack of knowledge) we have no idea what's going on.

The Presence of Grace

And so, as I say, the experience of expansion can seem devastating. Though you'll gain new friends, it's hard to let go of the old ones. Nevertheless, the name that we on the spiritual path give to this expansion is 'grace.'

What is grace? It can be seen as divine intervention in our personal affairs—God, sitting on his throne, occasionally (and all too arbitrarily, it often seems) bestowing wisdom on random innocents. Or we can regard it as the doings of a sort of "Grace Angel," whose only responsibility is to be on the lookout for likely candidates for grace. Another way to look at it is that somehow, from somewhere, a new dispensation comes upon us that wasn't previously available, and suddenly we know something we didn't know before. Or we feel a type of energy or emotion that was previously denied us—intense love for humanity, for example. It's certainly described in these terms often enough in the literature.

Perhaps all these definitions are true to one degree or another. But I would like to put it in the following way: Since Sufis believe that we are all a part of the being of

God, everything we do is also a part of God. Therefore, in doing what we do we are responding to an activity of the divine. We function in our capacity as part of the divinity, and we create a reality that, in our seemingly limited sphere, is appropriate to the divine purpose.

What I'm saying here is that *we are the purpose.* Sufis hold that all that exists is within us and is gradually unveiled. We already have the totality of knowledge within us but it has to be veiled from our consciousness; otherwise, it would interfere with our learning about physicality. The theory is that to the extent that it is our destiny to learn about such matters, more and more of this knowledge is revealed to us in living. The spiritual work we do is very much a part of this process. When we look at that work in this light, the sacrifices we make take on an entirely different character. They become a means of lifting the veil.

There is a tension in all of us between what we want to do with our lives and what the forces of society, which become interiorized, want us to do. The power of these forces can be such that we no longer know what we want. Our personal power is forged out of this tension—and the level of that depends on how courageous we are in taking on shifts in perception. If our commitment to illusion has been great, accepting these shifts may seem like a sacrifice.

People rarely plunge eagerly into shifting from one level of awareness to another. In fact, we in Sufism don't encourage such plunging. People responding to the inner call usually act timidly. They intinctively know that something big is about to happen, and they don't want to approach that something recklessly. "Besides," they tell themselves, "what seems to be a shift may just be a con." (There's no shame in having doubts. Pir Vilayat used to say it was silly to sacrifice your life savings for a con.)

What many of us think of as "divine dispensation"—the sudden seemingly miraculous intervention of God, a "Guardian Angel," or whatever—is really, as the Sufis see it, the universe's never-ending showering of compassion, mercy, spirit, peace and justice upon all of us. At a certain point, an internal switch is tripped in us and we begin to perceive and respond to this showering (perception and response being the same). The event may seem dramatic. We all love a drama. But human beings also love, and insist on, predictability. So when the divine dispensation—which was always there—suddenly and unexpectedly comes upon us, we often regard this spiritual windfall as an imposition, a sacrifice.

The new dispensation demands an entirely new response from us. We are free to accept or reject this. However, we tend to generate the old responses, since that is what we are so used to doing. The act of loving others, for example, can become a source of confusion, especially if we've always been selfish and demanding in expressing what we think is love.

Joy Is Real and Depression Is Not Inevitable

If our response to the world has previously been mainly one of depression, joy can be an even greater source of confusion. Depression is not inevitable. When people tell me they're depressed, I ask them what it feels like. Then I ask them what it feels like when they're not depressed. Usually, they can't remember. But if they're caught off guard, people who are clinically depressed can sometimes throw off their depression, at least temporarily. I've seen this happen, sometimes in the middle of Sufi dancing; then, the most profoundly depressed people can suddenly become responsive, expressive, joyful. Unfortunately, when the dancing stops they remember they're depressed. It's as if they deliberately re-gather a black cloud around themselves. They resume calling the state of darkness in which they live "the world."

I know depression can be difficult. I've been there myself. What brought me out of my depression—and this is one of the keys to getting out of depression—was deciding that the moments of joy we feel are real in themselves and not an escape from reality. It took me years and the sacrifice of what I considered to be a state of some profundity to emerge from depression. Now I know that this can be done just by deciding you're sick of feeling terrible. The only things you sacrifice are your wrong assumptions about reality.

Certainly chemical imbalance can play a role in depression. But if you have an insightful psychiatrist who successfully addresses the problem, then, once you've gotten yourself to a place of balance with the help of drugs, you can begin to examine your assumptions. I'm a firm believer in first addressing the symptoms, then the causes.

Pir-o-Murshid had a powerful saying that we in the Sufi Order International constantly quote, though we're careful about how and when we say it. The quote is: "Shatter your ideal on the rock of truth." Sacrifice indeed. What this statement means, at least in part, is that whatever you take to be real, usually isn't. Your belief in that reality will do for a time, but if you're paying attention, eventually it will have to give way to a more profound truth.

Don't assume you're so cool that all your ideals have already been shattered on the rock of truth. Nobody is that cool. We must all create ideals; they are the standards, the emblems of greater perfection toward which we strive. The guide/student relationship falls into this category of a created ideal, as do the details of your belief in God.

Most of us assiduously avoid acting on Pir-o-Murshid's admonition to shatter our ideals on the rock of truth. Perhaps that isn't the sort of thing you can do in a deliberate way. How would you know if you'd succeeded, anyway? But it's certainly within the power of us all to examine what we accept or believe, and then search for alternatives. The true shattering of an ideal is a matter of a deep, deep shift in knowledge. Otherwise, it is nothing but mere intellectual wheel-spinning.

15

Death

Death is a bridge whereby the lover rejoins the Beloved.

- RABIA

I grew up in a Protestant Christian household—Lutheran, to be exact. Looking back on it now, I would say that many of the people who thought of themselves as pious were actually merely self-righteous.

In my congregation death was explained as the point at which you either sank into the nether regions or were rewarded with eternal bliss. Eternal bliss sounded very dull. Spending eternity singing hymns sounded boring to a young lad bursting with energy. To me, this sort of bliss looked like the carrot leading you to behave properly, the stick being hell and damnation—really bad guys poking you with red-hot irons and delighting in your torment.

When I was still quite young I figured out that even singing boring hymns was better than getting poked with red-hot irons. As a teenager, though, I began to wonder if there might not be a third alternative.

My disenchantment with my church began innocently enough. In most religions, a teenager is required to attend a course of study. I highly recommend this. Although a child may be uninterested or even resentful at the time, a course of religious study teaches a child to think in religious terms. What is taught may be simplistic, but it's a useful experience that will be advantageous in later years, perhaps in surprising ways. So every Saturday morning, when I would much rather have been behaving more rambunctiously, I was taken by my parents to church and beleaguered with denominational propaganda. Believe it or not, for the most part I enjoyed the experience. I tend to accept whatever is unavoidable and do what I have to do to get through the experience.

So there I was with a group of other youthful captives, being taught the Lutheran perspective on living. My retreat from Christianity began during an innocent conversation we had with our pastor about obligation. The pastor explained that it is vitally important to seek salvation, emphasizing that once you are exposed to the Christian message—more specifically, to the Lutheran message—you must follow this path. If you do not, eternal damnation will be your lot.

I set before the pastor a hypothetical situation. A Hindu walks past a Christian storefront in India and notices the display in the window, say a cross or an effigy of Christ. The Hindu moves on without thinking anything further about it, not for the rest of his life. Is the Hindu then doomed to eternal damnation? The pastor said yes.

I said nothing, and pretended to accept what he had said. But in my innermost being it struck me that this was the dumbest thing I'd ever heard the pastor say. It was the beginning of the end of Lutheranism for me.

I discovered later that most if not all religious denominations are so steeped in doctrine that they've completely lost sight of the message of Christ that animated them in the first place. I suppose every institution eventually loses touch with the essence that formed it. At the time when I became upset with my pastor, I couldn't separate doctrine from essence myself. What really bothered me was that that perfectly innocent Hindu and all the other innocent people who walked past that Christian storefront were condemned to an eternity of damnation without knowing it, by a Lutheran pastor they'd never met and never even heard of. It seemed so blatantly silly that I was confused about it for years.

Death in the East and West

Sufis have clear and definite ideas about death, and those ideas are decidedly not Christian. Sufis regard death as nothing more than a door through which everyone must pass. Hazrat Inayat Khan writes,

> Death takes away the weariness of life, and the soul begins life anew. Death is a sleep from which the soul awakens in the hereafter. Death is the crucifixion after which follows the resurrection. Death is the night after which the day begins. It is death which dies, not life.

When you're young, death is an abstraction until somebody close to you dies. This is especially true in the Western world, where, when a human body stops functioning, it is regarded as merely something that must be dealt with in the most sanitary way possible. We've created whole institutions to help us avoid looking directly at death. But throughout most of human history the body of someone who had died was cared for by the family before it was buried, interred or cremated. It was washed, wrapped in cloths or clothed in finery, and then lowered into the earth, or entombed or burned. Now, when somebody dies, the body is efficiently whisked away by burial professionals who gently direct the relatives' every move while making reassuring noises. Hazrat Inayat Khan writes,

> We will not be afraid of death once we have discovered the true nature of the self. Once man has experienced the inner life, the fear of death has expired, because he knows death comes to the body, not to his inner being. When once he begins to realize life in his heart and in his soul, then he looks upon his body as a coat. If the coat is old he puts it away and takes a new one, for his being does not depend upon his coat. The fear of death lasts only so long as man has not realized that his real being does not depend on his body.

By our focus on merely sanitizing the process of death and burial, we've prevented ourselves from seeing what really goes on at a funeral. As a minister of the Sufi Order International, I'm sometimes called upon to officiate at funerals. Standing there in the funeral home, I've been able to observe the efficiency of burial professionals. I'm very aware that this is a business and that dealing effectively with the family is part of the business. But I'm also aware that even as the body of the dead person is lying there looking perfect, the soul of that person is hanging around trying to figure out what's happening. All too often, I have the experience of sitting in the mortuary waiting for the service to begin when I sense that the dead person's soul is in a state of confusion about what's going on. The confusion of the other people at the service further confuses the soul of the deceased.

We Americans no longer have any certainty regarding the assumptions our culture once held about death. Because we are loyal to a certain religion, we may subscribe to a certain attitude, but we can't help being aware that today there are other ways of looking at death and dying. People pay their respects to the dead even while wondering what's happening to that person's soul—or if that person has a soul. I'm convinced that much of the emotional turmoil at a wake or funeral is due to the very natural worry this situation evokes in us about the nature and outcome of our own dying. You can't help noticing that your friend or relative is lying very still. You know he or she won't be around to delight or bother you anymore. You can't help asking yourself, "So what's going to happen to me?"

Further confusing the issue is the increase in violent death in the world today, or at least the increase in our awareness of violent death. We know that at every moment, around the world, people are being gunned down or otherwise murdered, aimlessly or purposefully. We know it's very possible that one day we could end up looking down the wrong end of a gun barrel ourselves. A Romanian friend told me that during her country's transition from communism she and a friend were walking down a street in Bucharest when her friend was casually shot and killed by a sniper. There was no reason for this; it was offhand sniping taking place in the unrest of a transition period—people killing people just because they knew they could get away with it. You can imagine how deeply this senseless murder affected my Romanian friend. The experience persuaded her to find a way to come to the United States where she thought she would be safer. Everywhere in the world today, the increasing presence of violent death frightens and confuses us by its seemingly random nature.

Death in Life

Death is something of a puzzle for us all. We ask: What exactly *is* death? Does it truly extinguish what we are? Is there anything beyond death? If there is, what is it like?

Short of actually dying, there's only one way to find answers to these questions. That way is to go within. These days, many of us eagerly latch onto stories of near-death experiences. Such experiences take place within—that is, within the consciousness of the person who has seemingly died. The experience is being thought or dreamt. It is not an external one, but an internal one. "Near-death" experiencers see a tunnel or a white light but their eyes are closed; they are unconscious but they still touch or feel those who approach them. How do the experiencers manage this? They don't do it with their physical senses, though they still have the use of their bodies. They're so used to the reality of their bodies, that reality is still so compelling, that they cannot ignore it and so they experience these inner visions as if they were taking place in real life.

In the course of near-death experiences, the experiencers meet Mom or Dad or Uncle Albert, or perhaps a religious figure they're attached to; they converse with these entities and then return to their earthly bodies. Near-death isn't an experience you deliberately want to have, but we still sometimes envy persons who have it. They've experienced a reality that we are only told exists, and they've come back with a certainty that those of us who are more material-minded and matter-of-fact don't have.

The question is: How can we—without nearly dying!—acquire that degree of certainty?

Pir Vilayat was always extremely reluctant to talk about death, but when the subject came up he occasionally referred to his astral travels as having provided him with proof of life beyond life. He was reluctant to speak on this topic. He didn't want people to think that only through astral traveling—which not everyone can easily do—could the reality of an afterlife be established. He didn't want people to focus on astral travel.

In this he was correct. We don't need to astral travel to obtain knowledge of life after death. Many esoteric schools teach initiates to achieve a state—one quite difficult to achieve—in which the body is no longer important. If you arrive at this state, you find yourself adrift in a kind of cosmic sea of love or peace or serenity. The act of thinking is different there, because you are not limited by your synaptic impulses. In this state, it's not uncommon to think of your body as simply a conveyance you get in and out of or a suit of clothes you put on and take off. Until you've actually experienced it, you'll have to take the existence of this state on faith. But that existence is as real as that of the soul itself, of which Hazrat Inayat Khan said, "Verily, the soul has no birth, no death, no beginning, no end. Sin cannot touch it, nor can virtue exalt it; it has always been and always will be, and all else is its cover like a globe over the light."

The Passing of Michael

I've already talked about my friend Michael, a member of the Sufi Order International, who became terribly ill with stomach cancer. I've talked about how he rallied and fought and lived on for many more months than the doctors expected.

However, a little before noon on April 2, 2003, Michael made his transition to the next phase of existence. He had had a very difficult year, not only because of the chemotherapy, but also because his cancer was in his intestines and stomach and this had prevented him from eating for much of the time.

Nevertheless, Michael used his time well. During his last year I was with him as an observer, privileged to partially experience someone else's transformation. It occurred to me at the very end that over the past year he had, very slowly and with great intensity, been going through all the stages of a spiritual retreat. Michael had come to believe that knowing when he was going to die was a great gift. The knowledge focused his attention. It gave him the sort of deadline a personal retreat offers. I watched Michael ponder this journey, worry it, make sure he thoroughly knew each stage he was at before moving on to the next.

At one point I asked him where he was—I meant spiritually—and he replied that he was "just above Hobbitville." He wanted to know where that was. I told him he was probably emerging into the realm of consciousness the Sufis call *Mithal*, a dimension where metaphor and image take on a substantial reality. Scholars of Sufism call this plane of existence the "imaginal realm" (see Notes).

Michael liked the idea of being in *Mithal*. He hadn't known that such realms existed, probably because he'd always avoided the formal retreat process. On his last retreat he had ignored the practices and spent the entire six days drawing—and that retreat had been ten years ago. The nature of Michael's life was such that he was in a retreat space most of the time; probably he never needed to go through the formal process.

The soul is so much larger than our petty notions about it. Toward the end, those of us who were with Michael in his room didn't talk much; it was too fatiguing for him. What we did find ourselves doing was repeating, quite spontaneously, zikr (the remembering of God) "on the breath (i.e., silently)," each of us according to her or his own personal rhythm. Michael didn't say zikr with us. Mostly, he slept. As the rest of us silently remembered God, I noticed that the rhythms of our breathing were becoming one. We were having an experience of peace and joy and hope and reassurance, although we didn't talk about it at the time.

On Friday, April 2, 2003, the hospice nurse telephoned to tell me that Michael's time had come. I dropped what I was doing and drove straight to the hospital. I found Sharifa, Michael's wife, sitting in the darkened room holding her husband's lifeless hand. Michael had passed away.

The look on Sharifa's face as she sat there was very much like bliss. But as soon as she saw me the tears came.

She was sobbing quietly as I bent down to kiss her on the cheek. I forced myself to look at Michael's inert form lying on the bed. I restrained myself from leaning over to straighten a lock of his hair. Then I sat down wearily.

It was then that I noticed the distinctive atmosphere of the room. It was as if the heavens had opened out and all the great beings of the spiritual hierarchy were bending down over us. I was suddenly aware of Michael's joyful presence. I sensed that he had moved on, that he had gone home, and I suddenly wondered why we were all still crying.

Sharifa told me that when she'd seen Michael the night before, for the last time before he lost consciousness forever, his first words had been, "Good-bye. I have work to do." At the time Sharifa was taken aback. Now she knew what Michael had meant. A feeling almost of gratitude for his words was mingled with her grief.

I envied Michael in a way. He was finding out about a reality that those of us who have to carry on down here for a little longer encounter only in bits and pieces.

Since Michael's passing, I've wondered why I felt so little grief that night. He was, after all, one of my closest friends. Sharifa had had a similar reaction. We decided this was because we'd realized that night what had really happened to Michael; we knew where he had really gone. We'd done all our grieving at the beginning of his illness. Then we had watched as, over a period of a year, he had truly implemented the teachings of the Sufis.

Now Michael is having a good time, and we're still down here slogging away. I guess we should all start having a good time too.

16

So What Do I Do Now?

Every instant that the sun is risen,
if I stand in the temple, or on a balcony,
in the hot fields, or in a walled garden,
my own Lord is making love with me.   - KABIR

A friend read the manuscript of this book and said to me, "You aren't going to just stop there, are you?" When I asked her what more she wanted, she replied, "Well, I want to know what to do next. After I'm finished reading the book, then what?"

Good question. If only there were an easy answer.

The truth is, spiritual literature tends to oversimplify. "Okay, reader," it seems to say, "just follow these four rules/ these seven steps/ these eleven principles/ outlined in the book. Illumination will then be yours. At the very least, you will become very happy and contented."

It's easy for an author to say such things, and every reader wants to hear them. But the truth is more compli-cated. The fact is, each of us is a work in progress. We are compilations of all that we have experienced so far and the dim forms, emerging from potentiality, of all that we may experience in the future. Moreover, as Abi-Ru says in the preface, anything we read can only set us searching, not end our search. Words are static. Spiritual evolution is dynamic. What you read here may help you begin the quest, but it is not intended to—nor could it ever—walk you to your journey's end.

One of the most important Sufi insights is that each person is unique—not just in a murky "let's celebrate diversity" way, but truly and amazingly a unique manifestation of the One. Each path is an individual path; every spiritual journey is singular and distinct from every other.

Tempting as it is to lay down universal laws and commandments, Sufis resist that temptation. The Sufi philosophy is not a "one-size-fits-all" philosophy. As the great Persian Sufi poet Sa'adi wrote, "Every soul is born for a certain purpose, and the light of that purpose is kindled in his soul."

So, as a Sufi, I am reluctant to tell you what your next steps should be. On the other hand, I do like to talk. So I don't mind engaging in some speculation about what form those next steps might take.

Keep reading. If you've discovered that you are interested in the Sufi path, you are in luck—there are Sufi writings enough to fill a library. There are so many translations of Rumi, for instance, that you can choose your favorite flavor. Read—and think about what you're reading.

Take a class. Start to do yoga. Practice meditation. Once you have stepped firmly onto the spiritual path, you'll be surprised at how much company you have. If you're in a small town, explore the Internet. For starters, you might try these sites:

Sufi Order in the West: <http://www.sufiorder.org>
Website created by Pir Vilayat distilling his teachings into a series of meditation exercises: <http://www.universel.net>
Complete works of Hazrat Inayat Khan: <http://www.wahiduddin.net>
Books on Sufism & related topics: <http://www.omegapub.com>
Sufi Order in Europe events: <http://www.zenithinstitute.com>

Most important of all: Trust yourself. We are talking about your own individual path. Trust what you yourself feel is true about your experiences. Sure, we all want validation. We want someone—everyone!—to tell us, "Yes, that's a genuine spiritual experience. Now you're on the right track. Now you've got it!" It's natural to long for guidance and approval, but it's not necessary to have them. After all, when we share spiritual experiences, we are only describing our own personal universe and all its possibilities.

Even those of us who have been on the path for a while can forget to trust ourselves. Majida, my wife, was practicing an advanced breathing technique with a teacher. Suddenly, Majida found herself in a place beyond thought. This confused and disoriented her. She was sure she must be doing the exercise incorrectly. But when she told the teacher, the teacher replied: "Consider yourself blessed. You accessed a very rare state called 'intelligence without an object.'" Thinking over her teacher's words, Majida realized she had accessed this state many times before but had always dismissed the experience. She hadn't trusted herself enough.

Now that you've finished reading this book, you may feel that you are standing with your hand on the handle of a door that is still closed to you. You may be waiting for me to tell you to open that door, or maybe even waiting for me to tell you which way the handle turns. But you see, it's your door. It's your handle. It's your hand. Trust yourself. Trust your ability to learn. Trust the validity of your personal search. It's yours. Then, when you're ready, look for your guide. Until then—and ever after!—trust the Guide within you.

But remember to put your forehead to the floor from time to time.

NOTES

Introduction., p. 8, *Sayings*, 86

I, p. 19, *Blake*, 75/124

I, p. 21, *Gathas*, 223

I, pp. 24-25, *The Way*, 49

I, p. 27, *Sufi Teachings*, 62

II, p. 34, *The Way*, 50

II, p. 39, *Alchemy*, 251

II, p. 41-42, *Alchemy*, 165-166

III, p. 46, *Sayings*, 143

III, p. 51, Ibid., 165

IV, p. 59, *Le Droit de Seigneur*, Act 4, Sc.1

V, p. 71, *Sayings*, 33

V, p. 79, *Gita*, 122

VI, p. 98, *Sayings*, 69

VII, p. 100, *Awakening*, 6

VII, p. 102, Ibid., 7

VIII, p. 106, *Sayings*, 260

IX, p. 123, Ibid., 262

X, p.135, *Messages*, in unpublished works

X, p. 141, *Quran*, 908

XI, p. 146, *Unity*, 139

XI, p. 147, *Spiritual Liberty*, 144

XI, p. 150, *Unity*, 85

XII, p. 154, *Healing*, 114

XII, p. 159, *Sayings*, 68

XII, p. 163, Ibid., 104

XII, p. 165, Ibid., 80

XII, p. 167, Ibid., 90

XIII, p. 168, *Awakening*, 213

XIII, p. 172: In "Spiritual Liberty," Vol. V of the *Message* volumes, Murshid says: "According to Sufi tenets the two aspects of the supreme Being are termed Zat and Sifat, the Knower and the Known. The former is Allah and the latter Muhammad. Zat being only one in its existence, cannot be called by more than one name, which is Allah; and Sifat, being manifold in four different involutions, has numerous names, the sum of them all being termed Muhammad. The ascending and descending forms of Zat and Sifat form the circle of the Absolute. These two forces are called Nuzul and Uruj, which means involution and evolution. Nuzul begins from Zat and ends in Sifat; Uruj starts from Sifat and ends in Zat, Zat being the negative and Sifat the positive force. Zat projects Sifat from its own self and absorbs it within itself. It is a rule of philosophy that the negative cannot lose its negativeness by projecting the positive from itself, though the positive covers the negative within itself, as the flame covers the fire. The positive has no independent existence, yet it is real because projected from the real, and it may not be regarded as an illusion. Human ignorance persists in considering Zat to be separate from Sifat, and Sifat independent of Zat."

XIII, p. 173, *Gathas*, 202

XIII, p. 177, *Rumi*, 17

XIV, p. 180, *Sayings*, 109

XV, p. 192, Ibid., 99-100

XV, p. 193, *Inner Life*, 80

XV, pp. 196-197, *Sayings*, 67

XV, p. 198: Ibn 'Arabi writes: "*Alam al-Mithal* ('the imaginal realm'), which is also known as the realm of souls, is higher than the realm of the visible (*alam al-shahadat*) and lower than the realm of spirits. The realm of the visible is the shadow of the imaginal realm which, in turn, is the shadow of the realm of spirits. Everything that exists in this world exists also in the imaginal realm, that which is seen in dreams being a form of the imaginal realm. In the *Kashf al-Lughat* it states that the absolute imaginal realm is the realm of spirits, while the relative imaginal realm is the realm of imagination (*khayal*)." (Tahanawi [Nurbakhsh tr.], Kashshaf Istilahat al-Funun, 1342)

XVI, p. 200, *Kabir Book*, 56

About the Author

Phillip Gowins was born in Minneapolis, Minnesota, in 1945. He has been a cabinetmaker since 1980. In 1979, he met Pir Vilayat Inayat Khan and shortly thereafter was inducted into the Sufi Order in the West. A teacher in that order, he runs a Sufi Center at his home in Yonkers, New York, with his wife, Majida, who is also a teacher. Her daughter and their grandchildren live with them.

Phillip Gowins is available for workshops. To contact him, send an email to <Phillip_Gowins@hotmail.com>.

Selected Bibliography

Addas, C. *The Quest for Red Sulphur: The Life of Ibn 'Arabi.* Cambridge, England: Islamic Texts Society, 1993.

al-Ghazzali. *The Alchemy of Happiness.* Translated by Claud Field. Lahore, Pakistan: Sh. Muhammed Ashraf, 1964.

Arasteh, R. *Growth to Selfhood: The Sufi Contribution.* London: Routledge and Kegan Paul, 1980.

____. *Rumi, the Persian: Rebirth in Creativity and Love.* Tucson, AZ: Omen Press, 1972.

Armstrong, Karen. *The Battle for God.* New York: Alfred A. Knopf, 2000.

____. *A Short History of Islam.* New York: Modern Library, 2000.

Bayat, M. and M.A. Jamnia. *Tales from the Land of the Sufis.* Boulder, CO: Shambhala Publications, 1994.

The Bhagavad-Gita. New York, NY: Penguin Books, 1962.

Blake, Poetry and Prose of William. Edited by Geoffrey Keynes. London, England: The Nonesuch Library, 1956.

Burke, O.M. *Among the Dervishes.* New York: E.P. Dutton, 1975.

Chittick, W.C. *The Sufi Path of Knowledge.* Albany: State University of New York Press, 1989.

____. *The Sufi Path of Love: The Spiritual Teachings of Rumi.* Albany: State University of New York Press, 1983.

Ibn 'Arabi, M. *The Bezels of Wisdom.* Translated by R.W. J. Austin. New York: Classics of Western Spirituality, 1980.

Jami. *Yusuf and Zulaikha: An Allegorical Romance.* Edited, abridged and translated by David Pendlebury. London: Octagon, 1980.

Kabir. *The Kabir Book: Forty-Four of the Ecstatic Poems of Kabir.* Versions by Robert Bly. Boston: Beacon Press, 1977.

Khan, Hazrat Inayat. *The Alchemy of Happiness.* London, England: Servire, 1978.

____. *The Complete Sayings.* New Lebanon, NY: Omega, 1978.

____. *The Heart of Sufism: An Anthology.* Edited by Dr. H. J. Witteveen. Boulder, CO: Shambhala, 1999.

____. *The Inner Life.* Lebanon, NY: Omega, 1989.

____. *Sacred Readings: The Gathas.* Katwijk Aan Zee, The Netherlands: Servire BV, 1982.

____. *Spiritual Dimensions of Psychology (Collected Works).* Lebanon, NY: Omega, 1990.

____. *The Way of Illumination.* London, England: Barrie & Jenkins, 1973.

Khan, Vilayat Inayat. *Awakening: A Sufi Experience*. New York: Jeremy P. Tarcher/Putnam, 2000.

Moinuddin, Hakim. *The Book of Sufi Healing*. New York: Inner Traditions International, 1985.

Quran. Translated by A. Yusuf Ali. Washington, D.C.: Islamic Center, 1978.

Rumi, Jalal al-Din. *Crazy As We Are*. Translated by N. Ergin. Prescott, AZ: Holm Press, 1992.

___. *Rumi: Fragments, Ecstasies*. Translated by Daniel Liebert. Santa Fe: Source Books, 1981.

___. *Teachings of Rumi*. Ed. Andrew Harvey. Boston, MA: Shambala, 1999.

___. *Say I Am You*. Translated by John Moyne and Coleman Barks. Athens, GA: Maypop Press, 1994.

Shah, Idries. *Seeker After Truth*. London: Octagon Press, 1982.

van Stolk, S. and Daphne Dunlop. *Memories of a Sufi Sage: Hazrat Inayat Khan*. London: East-West Publications, 1990.

Vaughan-Lee, L. *Travelling the Path of Love*. Inverness, CA: Golden Sufi Center, 1995.

Vitray-Meyerovitch, Eva de. *Rumi and Sufism*. Translated by Simone Fattal. Sausalito, CA: Post-Apollo Press, 1987.

Index

THE NEWTON SERIES
Ancient Wisdom in the Modern World
Volume Two
The Sovereign Soul: Sufism: A Path for Today
by Phillip Gowins

Sir Isaac Newton (1642-1727) did not believe his great discoveries in physics and mathematics were new. He thought this knowledge was known to thinkers of the ancient world like Plato and Pythagoras. He believed these ideas had come into being long before the Flood, when they constituted part of a body of knowledge known in high antiquity as the *Prisca Sapientia*—the Pristine Wisdom.

Newton believed that knowledge of physical reality was only a part of the *Prisca*. He believed the Pristine Wisdom also contained knowledge of the soul of man. In numerous writings on alchemy, Biblical interpretation, Christian history and comparative mythology, Newton sought to reconstitute the part of the *Prisca Sapientia* that embodied this knowledge of the soul. He thought that originally this knowledge and that of physical reality had formed a single whole. His aim was to recreate the *Prisca Sapientia* in its entirety as a "unified field theory" of all knowledge. In doing so, he hoped to counteract the negative effects he foresaw would stem from a science shorn of spirituality; he sought to forestall the triumph of technology. Newton failed in his efforts to balance science with spirituality. He never completed his unified field theory.

The Sovereign Soul: Sufism: A Path for Today by Phillip Gowins is Volume Two of New Paradigm Books's NEWTON SERIES of books on Ancient Wisdom in the Modern World. Sir Isaac would have seen in the ritual dances of Sufism's whirling dervishes (which dances were meant in Rumi's time to emulate the movements of the planets) the descendent of the movements of the priests of ancient Egypt around a central fire (or "sun") in the worship ceremony Newton called the religion of the Prytaneum. Sir Isaac believed this religion had been brought by Noah through the Flood and that originally it was organically linked to the knowledge of the soul of man of the *Prisca Sapientia*. He would have seen in the beliefs and practices of the Sufis of today the survival of a profound body of spiritual knowledge going back to the beginnings of mankind. He would have welcomed the wisdom of the Sufis as one of a number of gentle correctives to the destructive effects of technology in the modern world.

Volume One of THE NEWTON SERIES of books on Ancient Wisdom in the Modern World is *In Search of the Unitive Vision: Letters of Sri Madhava Ashish to an American Businessman, 1978-1997,* compiled with a commentary by Seymour B. Ginsburg (New Paradigm Books 2001). It contains an account of the insights into the ancient knowledge of mankind of Sri Madhava Ashish and G. I. Gurdjieff.